"We set out firmly to tread the *inner way.*"

— Abba Macarius, Starets of Optino

# *Inner Way*

## Eastern Christian Spiritual Direction

JOSEPH J. ALLEN

WILLIAM B. EERDMANS PUBLISHING COMPANY
GRAND RAPIDS, MICHIGAN

255 Jefferson Ave. S.E., Grand Rapids, Mich. 49503


Printed in the United States of America

**Library of Congress Cataloging-in-Publication Data**

Allen, Joseph J., 1943-
Inner way: toward a rebirth of Eastern Christian spiritual direction / Joseph J. Allen.
p. cm.
Includes bibliographical references.
ISBN 0-8028-0695-3 (pbk.)
1. Spiritual direction. 2. Spiritual formation — Orthodox Eastern Church.
3. Orthodox Eastern Church — Doctrines. I. Title.
BX382.5.A55 1993
253.5′3′088215 — dc20 93-46990
CIP

This book is dedicated to my father in Christ,
Metropolitan PHILIP Saliba
and
with love and gratitude to Valerie Marie, Phillip and Joseph
for their patience which extended far beyond this book,
to Refa Zouzoulas for her many hours of typing the text,
to Paul Garrett for the important task of technical editing,
to Edward Huenemann for his brotherly consultation,
and especially to the many who have invited me to traverse with
them the *inner way* toward God and each other.

# Contents

# Preface

To ENTER the *inner way* is risky, dangerous — one can even say "fearful." There are a multitude of reasons why this is so. Most of all, it is fearful because it represents an encounter of spiritual depth, one which not only leads to a deeper relationship among human persons, but also seeks to carry us to the very root of all relationships — the presence of the living God himself. In the *inner way* one learns what the scripture means: "It is a fearful thing to fall into the hands of the living God" (Heb. 10:31). Such an encounter — which influences every other encounter in life — requires much on the part of both spiritual director and directee. This is the story of that encounter.

From the outset the reader should know that the writer of this work comes out of the Eastern Christian tradition. Spiritual direction was born in the Christian East, and has had a a strong impact on the spirituality of the Eastern Churches. However, it has been written for the benefit of Christians of both the West (Roman Catholics and Protestants) and the East (the various Eastern and Oriental Orthodox Churches).

The reader should also understand the structure of our exploration as reflecting the very nature and practice of spiritual direction. To begin, spiritual direction is a *ministry,* but one which requires an understanding of its particular *history,* a proper application of *theology,* and a grasp of the *psychology.* Taken together, these emerge within a concrete *methodology.* The meaning of these words forms the general outline of this book. Chapter One introduces the historical figure of the "Spiritual Physician" who practiced this ministry, and whose goal was

— and remains today — the reconciliation of the directee with God and neighbor. In Chapter Two we will delve deeper into the history of the "elder" in order to uncover the central characteristics of this ministry across time. On the basis of these findings, then, we will move to its contemporary practice as we examine in separate chapters both aspects of the term "spiritual direction": the *spiritual* component (or the theological roots) in Chapter Three, and the *direction* component (or the appropriate psychology and methodology) in Chapter Four. In an appendix we briefly note how four practitioners of direction have integrated this history, theology, and psychology in the task of this ministry.

If entering the *inner way* is fearful — and it is — it must also be said that the gains realized by the person willing to risk it are *immense.* In truth, there is no other way in life to realize such gains than to take that risk.

JOSEPH J. ALLEN

# Foreword

IS THERE such a thing as a decent human being? With those words a Norwegian ambassador confronted me in our first conversation in South Africa. He was on his last assignment after thirty-two years in his government's diplomatic service. Based on his experience in international relations, his judgment on the prospect for humanity wavered between cynicism and hope. His scepticism was not unfounded.

In a sense, this study of spiritual direction, according to the Eastern Christian tradition (from whence it comes), raises this same question regarding the "decent human being." As Father Joseph Allen writes, however, this is a struggle which is entered only if one is willing to traverse the "inner way." Today many of us, like my Norwegian friend, waver between cynicism and hope; we know the reason for scepticism. Neither the global scene nor our inner response to it is reassuring. Uncertainty besets and incapacitates us. Without spiritual direction the weakness of the flesh threatens to disable us.

Awareness of the peril which confronts both societies and individuals has, indeed, led some like Father Allen to probe the roots which nourish the human spirit. This quest has prompted religious revival on many fronts, but the anxiety which instigates the quest has all too frequently turned the renewal of religion toward fanatical and fundamentalist expression. Instead of an increase in humanity, gross inhumanity has marked the resurgence of religion. The light of religious promise is turned to darkness, which makes the future appear more grim than ever. Religious warfare is still a twentieth-century reality!

After years of struggle toward liberation and the opportunity "to be and do," the question "to be and do *what*" goes largely unanswered. Without a sense of commitment and purpose, without clarity of direction, the human spirit explodes and self-destructs. A sense of hope, or purpose, or meaning, or direction is absent and the energy for living wasted. This study seeks to enter the "what" into the formula of being and doing.

We know, however, that the recovery of a "decent human being" requires more than a struggle for liberation on the one hand or restriction by religious fanaticism on the other. The shaping of a decent human life is the disciplined use of freedom for ultimate purpose. In religious terms, this means the assumption of theological (i.e., discerning and not merely religious, pious, or passionate) responsibility toward God and our neighbor. In specifically Christian terms it means discipleship. It means getting our life together as followers and sisters and brothers of Jesus the Christ, *the* decent human being.

That a priest of the Orthodox Church of Antioch who is familiar with the early and later tradition of spiritual direction in the Eastern church has set out to explore the "inner way" and share his understanding may well prove a major contribution to the ecumenical discourse in our time. We in the West have often accused the Eastern church of being too quietist and mystical and not activist and relevant enough. What we may be discovering in all our activism and struggle for relevance is the prior need for a deeper spirituality in a "knowledge of the heart." The genuineness of our humanity and our sensitivity is sometimes in doubt. Our evangelism, our witness to the Gospel, has too frequently been marked by arrogance and the baptism of Western power. Our spiritual direction has too often been determined by economic, political, and social advantage in a competitive world where the lust for power has become a threat to the power of love. We suspect our souls may be in jeopardy.

The classical and especially Eastern tradition of Christianity has known the importance of self-examination and the "inner way." So seriously was this pursued that no one was condemned to going the way alone. As Father Joseph indicates, the subapostolic church honored the central role of "elders," spiritual leaders, both for the sake of the commuity as a whole and the spiritual welfare of each individual in it. Though their psychological and sociological tools may have been limited, their theological sensitivity made them aware of the fact that the shaping of human life, discipleship, and discipline could not be left to chance or indifference. The community and the individuals in it needed the ministry of those who had learned wisdom and compassion through struggle along the inner way. Such a ministry of eldership could be a boon to the humanization and community-building functions of churches today which exist in a depersonalized and bureaucratized society.

Especially Western Calvinists (both self-identified and non-self-conscious heirs) whose ecclesiastical structure focuses on the role of elder could recover a sense of what that might mean both in and beyond the believing community. John Calvin, like one of his chief mentors, John Chrysostom, knew the significance of spiritual direction and discipline in the ecclesiological and ecclesiastical life of the believing community. Neither John Calvin nor his mentors believed that ecclesiastical bureaus or "governing bodies" were anything more than instruments for the external ordering of common life. What was central to the life of the church was "spiritual direction," a "knowledge of the heart," which made life in communion with God and the neighbor possible. It is of more than passing interest that John Calvin had his own crest inscribed with the words "my heart I give thee, O Lord, gladly and sincerely." Such commitment is the essence of Orthodox spirituality, as this exploration shows.

Father Joseph Allen's study could well help Western Christians of "the word" learn to enter more fully into the spiritual life of the "inner way." Abraham Heschel, the noted Jewish philosopher, remarked many years ago that "Western civilization will be in difficulty as long as we believe that words are only referents to things. Words are vehicles of the human spirit." Neither verbal literalism nor totally irrational spiritualism will offer the direction which can make the "inner way" to decent humanity possible. In fact, it was a significant Calvinist theologian of the nineteenth century who complained that many of his contemporary fellow pastors spoke "the words of truth but not the truth of the words." There is more to life than superficial adherence which tries to live to the letter.

It is the "truth of the words" which this book invites us to explore. The author moves from the insights of the New Testament and the early church to contemporary insights informed by the psychology and sociology of knowledge. The text is an extended plea for the restoration of the ministry of "the elder," a ministry which serves people along the "inner way" and helps them find spiritual direction.

Western readers, especially Protestants, will find some basic anthropological assumptions foreign to their heritage. Father Joseph does not share the Western concept of the sinful nature of human beings as espoused by those Calvinists who understand the doctrine of "total depravity" as descriptive of the essential nature of people. Nor does his acceptance of the Orthodox doctrine of "theosis" (deification, i.e., true humanity is realized only in relationship with the divine prototype of humanness) easily square with Western traditions of sanctification, either Roman Catholic or Protestant.

It is, however, precisely these differences in anthropological assumptions which will challenge most Western readers to give their presuppositions "one distillation the more" (Kierkegaard), as they seek to engage in a ministry of spiritual direction with each other as companions on the way. By such critical reflection they may discover theological insights which psychology and sociology as secular tools do not by themselves provide. A more adequate and complete vision of the decent human being may come to light for all who seek spiritual direction on the inner way. Certainly such a mutual quest by those holding either Eastern or Western assumptions could be rewarding.

May this author's plea be heard in churches and theological seminaries. The recovery of a clearer vision of a "decent human being" and a more disciplined effort to discover our spiritual direction could bring us all close to a true "people's theology," in which the heart of the matter is known, and cause many to rejoice.

Edward Huenemann, Th.D.
*Director, The Theology in Global Context Association*

# 1 Treading the Inner Way: A Ministry of Healing and Reconciliation

*God, who has reconciled us to himself through Christ . . . has given us the ministry of reconciliation.*

2 Cor. 5.18

## 1. *Iatros Pneumatikos:* The Spiritual Physician

There is a distinct and personal history to the present exploration of spiritual direction. I was born and raised in the Eastern Christian tradition, and have for many years taught in various theological schools according to that tradition. In my years of teaching I have discovered, however, that in theological schools of *all* faiths, many class hours are devoted to this subject by young students and seminarians nearing the end of their formal training, those who will soon enter the practice of Church ministry in one form or another — either as clergy or lay workers. It is my experience that this subject requires greater intensity and resolution than any other course in the area of the pastoral ministry — and for no small reason: *first,* because spiritual direction in one shape or another has always formed a central component in Christian living; *second,* because it has for too long been either secularized or simply neglected among the laypeople of all Christian traditions, and we can even say especially in the Eastern tradition in which it finds its very roots; and *third,* because it can be — and should be — a crucial mode for "doing ministry" in today's world. It is clear that a reawakening is needed in spiritual direction.

Paradoxically, although this ministry was born in the Christian East, a renewal in the *practice* of spiritual direction mostly continues in the West, particularly in the Roman Catholic and Anglican communions.[1] In the course of this Western renewal, however, some obvious changes have been made to those "classical forms" which were born in the deserts of Egypt and the Middle East, and later transplanted into Russia and Eastern Europe. It was in Eastern Europe, as we shall see in the literature, where spiritual direction blossomed as a vibrant tradition — and then faded. Indeed, this being the case, those in the Eastern tradition today can both contribute to — and learn from — that renewal of its practice worldwide as we *all* resolve to join Abba Macarius in "setting out firmly to tread the *inner way.*"

The various concerns in the study of spiritual direction in a distinct Christian setting cluster around the question: "How can we direct (guide, counsel) those persons entrusted by God to our care in such a way as to remain rooted in the Apostolic Christian tradition, and yet not fail to make proper use of the many contemporary resources — sociological, anthropological, physiological, and psychological — which are available to us?" In understanding this question, we begin to approach the important place in the ministry of the Church of the *iatros pneumatikos,* the "spiritual physician." Students preparing to undertake this ministry quickly realize that the historical pattern and paradigm for the task is found in the study of the *elder* ("γέρων" [*gerōn*] in Greek; "*starets*" in the Slavic tongues; "*abba*" and "*imma*" — "father" or "mother" — in the Semitic tongues) which is so solidly rooted in Eastern Christianity. As will become evident in this study, such eldership, regardless of "titles," must be today a concern for all Christian communities, not only those of the Christian East. But this ancient ministry must somehow be linked to contemporary circumstances. How is the person who gives himself or herself to the ministry of spiritual direction

1. Useful monographs include: John T. McNeill, *A History of the Cure of Souls* (New York: Harper & Row, 1951); Kenneth Leech, *Soul Friend* (San Francisco: Harper & Row, 1977); Thomas Hart, *The Art of Christian Listening* (New York: Paulist Press, 1980); and Thomas Merton, *Spiritual Direction and Meditation* (Collegeville, MN: Liturgical Press, 1960). Articles: Ivan M. Kontzevitch, "Eldership," *Epiphany Journal* 9.4 (Summer, 1989), 35-44; and Kevin Albert Wall, O.P., "Direction, Spiritual," *New Catholic Encyclopedia* (New York: McGraw-Hill, 1976), 4.887-90.

to draw from *both* universes? How can one remain rooted in Christian tradition and yet benefit from contemporary discovery?

In any academic study and in lectures in spiritual direction one must draw materials from a broad spectrum: scripture, ethics, history, literature, the arts, human experience, cultural factors, etc. Such an academic exploration quickly leads the student beyond the historical study of the spiritual director, a term which, after all, has been applied to a very few individuals chosen to practice this very exacting "science and art"[2] — as "spiritual physicians" (ἰατροὶ πνευματικοί [*iatroi pneumatikoi*]).[3] While most of the classical spiritual physicians were monastic elders — and here is where we move beyond the bounds of that history — *spiritual direction has never been strictly synonymous with the elder of the past* — and must not be today. It is unfortunate that some people advocate such a total *identification*. Perhaps the chief lesson to be learned from history is that spiritual direction must be brought to bear on the circumstances facing the people of God in *any* era — including our own. This can be done only if we understand spiritual direction as a *ministry* which can never be relegated to history; it must be something always happening today, because ministry is what the Church *does*.

2. See St. Gregory Nazianzen, *In the Defence of his Flight to Pontus,* in *Nicene and Post Nicene Fathers of the Christian Church,* Series 2.7.203-27 (hereafter cited as *NPNF*). St. Gregory calls this practice "the art of arts, and the science of sciences" (p. 208). See also St. Gregory of Rome, *Pastoral Rule* 1 in *Ancient Christian Writers,* 11 (New York: Paulist Press, 1950), 21. St. Gregory refers to the "direction of the souls" as the "art of arts" *("ars est artium regimen animarum").*

3. Since spiritual direction is always an effort to *heal* the person, the traditional literature is replete with titles which utilize medical terminology. This usage was already firmly rooted in ancient Greek philosophy, where healing was seen occurring through the "sage" who guided the person into the inner life. Thus, Socrates saw himself as an ἰατρὸς τῆς ψυχῆς (*iatros tēs psychēs:* "soul healer"). St. Anthony of Egypt, the father of monasticism, says, "The fathers of old went into the desert, and when they were made whole, they became physicians, and returning again they made others whole; therefore it is said, 'Physician, heal thyself'" (*The Desert Fathers [Apophthegmata Patrum],* ed. Helen Waddell [London: Collins, 1972], 147). Abba Apollo, in the same source, is quoted as stating that when a spiritual father asks questions in order to give counsel, he is like "a wise physician" (75). Certain texts in the canonical literature utilize similar terminology. More recently, St. John of Kronstadt in Russia referred to the priest engaged in spiritual direction as "a spiritual physician to whom you can show your wounds without shame . . . trusting and confiding in him" (*The Spiritual Counsels of Father John of Kronstadt,* ed. W. Jardine Grisbrooke (Crestwood, NY: St. Vladimir's Seminary Press, 1967), 122. Additional instances of medical terminology are provided in the text.

Our understanding of this issue is closely linked with our understanding of Christian *pneumatology:* that the Holy Spirit abides in every age, passes beyond the walls of any church, and, as St. Paul notes, is the very source of *all* the "gifts of ministry" (see Rom. 12.6 and 1 Cor. 12), including that of spiritual direction. Hence, we must perceive the same Holy Spirit as having provided the contemporary Church with forms other than those used by the ancient elder to achieve this same purpose. We see this in the various "father confessors" and other spiritual guides, clergy and lay. Even if one were to claim that "there is not one Elder remaining on the face of the earth,"[4] it would be wrong to go on to claim that the Spirit of God could not again, in any age, raise up the *patēr pneumatikos* (the spiritual father) for the continuing ministry of the Church. But since the Spirit *does* abide in the Church, it follows that there *will* be an ever-renewing form of πνευματοφόροι [*pneumatophoroi*] — "bearers" or "carriers" of that Spirit. Therefore, although spiritual direction may have been born in the historical ministry of the elder, and may even have reached its richest expression thus far in that ministry, it must never be relegated to the shelves of dead history — which is what happens when spiritual direction is so radically identified with a particular form from the past.

Once we have clarified this point, those of us who teach in this area discover that our classes are free to move beyond the parameters of historical context and break out into the more global concerns of Christian living. But every year I am surprised anew at having to wrestle with this issue — particularly since the very content of this "science and art," even in its distinct historical setting, shows that the goal of spiritual direction has always been the same as that of the Gospel itself: to lead individuals deeper and deeper into the struggle for the Christian life, that is, toward wholeness and healing. And this remains its central task today. Furthermore, this task is central whether or not the life of the person being directed is currently undergoing a crisis.

Spiritual direction has always included, at one time or another, those elements relative *both* to the daily struggle for wholeness and healing, and to a proper ongoing prayer life. Here it should be emphasized that spiritual direction has never concerned itself with the person's "rule of prayer" without also dealing with the thoughts and actions (somatic, psychological,

4. See Archimandrite Chrysostomos, ed., *Obedience* (Brookline, MA: Holy Cross Press, 1984), 44.

sociological, etc.) of his or her everyday life. It was the person's experience as a whole which became the very content of dialogue with the director. As one was led toward a deeper communion with God, there was always a focus on what was operational *within* oneself — the perceptions of heart and mind — and *between* oneself and God and his or her fellows — behavioral concerns. Christian communion depends on these two experiential elements. It is through a shared interpretation — a "life-hermeneutic" — of one's experiences that the spiritual physician has always aimed at awakening in believers the truth regarding their motivations and predicaments. History reveals that the direction given was sometimes gentle, sometimes radical, sometimes even brutal; as we will see, examples of each abound in the stories of the *Apophthegmata Patrum,* a very early and classic collection of the "sayings" of the fathers of the desert. No matter how direction was imparted, though, it never avoided or denied the real, operative factors of an individual's circumstances, whether they were evaluated as positive or negative, constructive or destructive. In short, were truth denied, no healing could have occurred.

But what has the director traditionally used to form his evaluations? He has always based his direction on the Christian anthropology in which he was rooted, and measured everything in life against its paradigm: the *Theanthrōpos* himself — the God-man, Christ Jesus. We shall return to the question of anthropology in spiritual direction, for it is one of the marks which distinguishes its Christian practice from other forms of counsel and guidance.

Year after year, students and seminarians discover anew the inclusivity of this very rich — but also very risky — form of ministry. It deals with all that a person is and does before the face of God. But sooner or later in the course of such lectures, students will push their instructors to present a *modus,* a vehicle, which will allow them, today, to grab onto this form of ministry. And — *mirabile dictu!* — they discover that it is in the *mystery of a relationship* and in the *sharing of a story* that this lies. The academic course which begins with an historic exploration of the exact "science and art" of the spiritual physician, ends with the lesson that distinctly Christian spiritual direction is a process whereby one individual — the director — is welcomed into the life-story of another — the directee — past, present, and future. The directee enters a relationship of trust with his or her director, and the latter agrees to walk with that person on his or her "faith journey" through life. "Relationship" and "story" are key words in the study of spiritual direction.

Seen in this way, then, the spiritual director is like a "literary critic" who, through a relationship of intimacy and trust, helps another Christian to "write" his or her life story. This he does by delving into the various chapters which are already "written," while never neglecting the unfolding present story. This, in turn, equips him to help the directee, by God's grace and that person's own goodwill, to write the continually unfolding future chapters — all, of course, in an atmosphere of sincere prayer.

As we shall soon discover, every person's story contains a multitude of characters, images, and actions, each of which has made an impact — positive *or* negative — on it and has helped to shape it. These influences may be carried into the person's present story from the past, or may be most active in the present; in either case, they may well seek to lead that story in a particular direction in the future. Whatever influences may mark the story, the distinctly Christian approach to spiritual direction will be to influence deeper communion with God. This is, indeed, the chief hallmark of any Christian ministry.

## 2. A Question of Contemporary Ministry

To study spiritual direction is to study one of the varieties of ministries which has been given to the Church by God (1 Cor. 12.4-5). But the study of any ministry through the course of history will inevitably reveal a diversity of terms, emphases, and intentions. Thus, at one time the very term "ministry" might be understood in both the Western and Eastern Churches primarily to refer to an "office" (bishop, presbyter, deacon); at another, it might conjure up the varied functions of "all the people of God," clergy and laity alike; at still other times, it might suggest the exacting functions of "apostles, preachers, teachers," as in the sub-apostolic Church.

However, in whatever form the term is used, ministry has always been known as one of the "gifts" (χαρίσματα [*charismata*]) of God's grace: having "gifts that differ according to the grace given to us," Paul enjoins, let us use them (Rom. 12.6-8). Thus, the ministry of spiritual direction must be seen as something precisely to be *used.* As early as the second century, St. Irenaeus of Lyon emphasized this truth:

> Those who are truly his disciples receive grace from him and put this grace into action for the benefit of others, each as he has received the gifts. There is simply no limitation to the gifts which, all over the world, the Church has received from the Lord, and put into action day by day, in the name of Christ Jesus. . . . For as the Church has freely received from the Lord, so it freely serves humankind.[5]

Looking closely at these words, one notes that both "grace" and "gifts" refer to the dynamic nature of ministry. It is at once "received" and "offered" — received from the Lord in order to be offered: "put into action for the benefit of others . . . day by day." No better definition of ministry could be given; it is always — and only — a "service" given by God and delivered to others. Indeed, throughout history this has been the central orientation and true content of the Church's διακονία [*diakonia*], ministry.

By definition, then, spiritual direction must include the components common to all ministries: given by God and used for others. But given to whom? And used in what way? On these points there is considerable debate. For example, some propose that the term "spiritual direction" has no place in contemporary ministry; it is solely a relic of the past. Others claim that it is nothing more than "pastoral counsel"; the term "direction" should be avoided. Others seek to demonstrate its intimate connection with and evolution into the modern role of "father confessor." Still others argue that it is vital to be scrupulous about terminology (and usually exalt the particular role of the monastic elder above all others).[6] It is my own opinion that spiritual direction is a much needed "gift" from God which *must* be reawakened.

If we are to seek this "reawakening," however, we must begin by investigating the historical genesis and development of spiritual direction. As we do, we will learn that there are certain dimensions of its practice which serve to differentiate it from other present-day forms of counsel and care, and others with which it shares common elements. It should be quickly added that I do not intend here to study history *as such* — or canon law, as such; or liturgical practice, as such — but will limit the dimensions of my study to the core of the διακονία [*diakonia*] of the Church.

5. Cited in *The Early Christian Fathers,* ed. Henry Bettenson (London: Oxford University Press, 1974), 93.

6. Chrysostomos, *Obedience,* 43-47.

The study of this ministry will inevitably raise issues of "appropriation." How are we today to appropriate the forms about which we will learn from history in order to serve the needs of contemporary believers? We are standing at the juncture between the past and present. It is always easier — and less risky — to deal with the past; the facts are in and recorded. It would be naïve to pretend, however, that new things are not constantly being learned, that such newer understandings are not important, or that none of these ought to be pressed into our contemporary *praxis* of spiritual direction. How fitting are our Lord's words in the Gospel:

> Therefore every scribe who has been trained for the kingdom of heaven is like the master of a household who brings out of his treasure what is new and what is old. (Mt. 13.52)

The truth is that no matter what approach one takes with regard to the exact place and usage of the term "spiritual direction," one can hardly disagree that, even if one cannot practice it as the precise science and art of the ancient elder, one certainly can — and *must* — apply to the Church's current task the rich heritage of the inner way. Though the specific problems and challenges we face in life today may differ from those of ages past, still the human search and yearning for healing and wholeness which has always marked sincere persons in every age continues to mark them in the present — and will for the remaining future.

Even if history's sad lesson is that *not everyone has sought spiritual direction,* still there have always been some people who have searched for the *inner way,* and in doing so, have seen fit to seek out others who could direct them toward Christian healing and wholeness. Can it be any different today? Jesse Trotter states the challenge:

> "The glory of God is a person fully alive." So wrote Irenaeus in the second century. Yet look about you. How many people seem to be busily contriving to stay *half*-well, *half*-alive? So we overwork, oversmoke, overeat, and overdrink.[7]

"Wholeness has some fear in it for us," according to Trotter. To move forward on the path to wholeness, toward a oneness with God and our

7. Jesse Trotter, *Christian Wholeness: Spiritual Direction for Today* (Wilton, CT, Morehouse-Barlow, 1982), ix.

neighbor, whoever that might be, is to experience inner freedom. But this might be precisely what we are trying to avoid! He cites Kierkegaard: "Does the prospect of a genuine inner freedom make us anxious? 'Anxiety is the dizziness of freedom.'"[8]

Trotter goes on to explicate the need for applying the deep lessons of spiritual direction to contemporary ministry:

> We are the cleverest of all animals. If, in fact, wholeness does threaten us, we can run from wholeness, which also beckons us, in every possible direction. We can "run away *forward*" into work, *backward* into tranquilizers, *upward* into fantasy, *downward* into depression, *sideways* into evasion and avoidance. All to avoid the wholeness for which something else in us so hungrily longs.[9]

Wholeness, then, is what we seek. But this is not a condition distinct from the universal goal of the Christian spiritual life — or the ministry which nourishes it. Indeed, both wholeness and holiness are derived from the same Greek word, ὅλος [*holos*], and this common derivation is important, in that it emphasizes the human yearning for unity — for oneness and communion. For the Christian, such a longing for wholeness is always a yearning for God, but finds expression both in relations with one's neighbors and within one's self: the ministry of the Church in general seeks to achieve this.

As Trotter emphasizes, this is particularly important for us today, in a time that is increasingly fragmented and inwardly broken. Of course, there have always been impediments to spiritual growth, the various negative blocks which both can arise within a person and can come upon him or her from outside. These can range from any of the plethora of human evils and sins which press in upon our lives, and which seek to find a habitation within us, to the mere fact of human limitation, which we are so often unwilling to accept. Any one of these — and more — can misdirect us from the spiritual development proper to a Christian.

What we need — what has always been needed — is a process capable of leading us through the impediments toward that wholeness which is *natural* to human life. Here it is helpful to turn to the Eastern Christian tradition which, unlike an Augustinian approach which has

8. *Ibid.*
9. *Ibid.*

marked the West, has always emphasized that it is most natural for humankind to be "linked" to the presence of God, in communion with him. Following this line of thought, assuming that that linkage is natural, the task of the ministry of spiritual direction thus becomes seeking *reconciliation:* by removing the various obstacles which have led us astray into *alien* life paths, we open up the *natural* path, the inner way which leads to God.

*Any* Christian ministry must be transparent to Christ's own work, as the Apostle Paul states: "God, who reconciled us to himself through Christ . . . has given us the 'ministry of reconciliation' [διακονία τῆς καταλλαγῆς]" (2 Cor. 5.18). Spiritual direction, as a particular form of ministry, must concentrate on this primary task given to us by God. If, as Christ's disciples, we have truly received this grace from God, must we not today follow St. Irenaeus's example and ask ourselves: "How shall we put this grace into operation for the benefit of others?" This is a crucial question if we hope to restore the ancient practice of spiritual direction to its proper place in today's church.

## 3. Reconciliation through Appropriation

Because spiritual direction cannot be understood outside the global task of the Church's "ministry of reconciliation," we must examine this larger sense of mission — particularly understood in the Eastern Christian tradition. St. Basil the Great, for example, describes the Church's ministry primarily in terms of the ἐπιμέλεια [*epimeleia*] or "encompassing care," which its ministers are called to administer, mirroring the Lord himself, who is both "the shepherd [ποίμενος: *poimenos*] and guardian [ἐπίσκοπος: *episkopos*]" of our souls (1 Pet. 2.25).

St. Basil focuses attention on the *person* and *function* of the προεστώς [*proestōs:* leader] within the given Christian community.[10] He views this particular ministry as applying — or appropriating — the inherited faith and theology to the particular circumstances which he finds locally. The Greek term which he uses for this process is instructive: περίπτωσις

10. See Joseph J. Allen, *The Ministry of the Church: Image of Pastoral Care* (Crestwood, NY: St. Vladimir's Seminary Press, 1986). These terms are explained in Chapter 3 (pp. 69-95).

[*periptōsis:* embracing]; the agenda and parameters for how the moral guidance inherent in theology is to be "accommodated" to specific conditions is determined by those conditions — it is to embrace them.[11] While the essence and central meaning of the apostolic faith is constant and eternally unchanging, the conditions of human life do change.

We find the paradigm for this dynamic of appropriation in the very person of God himself. Eastern Christian theology teaches that God is always as he is — eternally congruent — and yet able to "accommodate" himself to our humanity in accomplishing his ministry to us.[12] Was this not what occurred in the Incarnation? In allowing himself to be "wrapped in swaddling clothes, laid in a manger" — that is, wrapping himself in our human condition, through our human flesh — did he not "accommodate" himself to our condition "for our sake and for our salvation?" And in doing so, he remained "true God of true God." The Incarnation and subsequent earthly life of Jesus — as well as the gift of the Holy Spirit which he sends from the Father to abide in us — are these not expressions of God's ministry to us? Has God not appropriated his own life — his Word — to us in order to bring about our reconciliation? Are his Word and Spirit not the "hands" by which God makes himself available to us — graspable? St. Gregory Nazianzen described the divine action in succinct and striking terms: "The Creator bows down to his own creation; the King of the heavens submits himself to the servant of the earth." We find this same emphasis in St. Paul's ode to Christ's humility: "Let the same mind be in you that was in Christ Jesus, who, though he was in the form of God, did not regard equality with God as something to be exploited, but emptied himself, taking the form of a slave, being born in human likeness" (Phil. 2.5-7). If Christ himself, the ultimate Spiritual Physician, could practice appropriation in his ministry, so too must we, as we reflect his work in the world.

11. See Stanley Harakas, *Toward the Transfigured Life* (Minneapolis, MN: Light and Life Publishing, 1983), 10-15. Harakas explains these important terms from the perspective of the history of ethics, but they are no less valid here. For example, the "*exomologētaria*" were a collection of guidelines in book form to provide ethical directives for use by father confessors in hearing confessions *("exomologēsis")*. Says Fr. Harakas (pp. 12-13): "The 'Periptosiologia' (*Periptōsis* in Greek means the 'circumstance' and thus the application of the moral rule to the specific cases) tended to become legalistic in the West. . . ." In the East, they were more used as theological guidelines.

12. See Thomas Oden, *Kerygma and Counseling* (New York: Harper & Row, 1978), 56-59. The author uses the term "Divine Congruence" in making his point.

St. Basil's "total care," however, does not fuse into one the distinctive functions of ministry in the Church; nor has the *proestōs* historically been free to appropriate theology outside certain *modes* of application set by the Church. Within the context of his overall call by God to maintain a most intimate and compassionate relationship with those entrusted to him — "he calls his own sheep by name . . . and the sheep follow him because they know his voice" (Jn. 10.2-4) — those assigned the ministry of reconciliation find themselves operating in three general modes which bear examination.

The first mode is that of λειτουργός [*leitourgos:* the "liturgist"].[13] Writing from the Eastern tradition, I give this liturgical function priority for a variety of reasons. At the popular level, because worship is the most visible form of ministry, providing the wealth of blessings, services, and celebrations which mark the lives of all Christians. Theologically, the *leitourgos* — or "minister in the sanctuary" to whom the scriptures refer (Heb. 8.2) — performs a crucial part of leading the faithful to reconciliation. In Eastern theology, it has always been emphasized that reconciliation and communion with God are most fully realized in the sacramental life — and the Eucharist in particular. In celebrating the services, the priest in the Eastern Church [ἱερεύς: *hiereus*], as *leitourgos,* does not act on his own, but "presents" to the community the One *Leitourgos* — Christ himself, the "minister in the sanctuary and the true tent that the Lord, and not any mortal, has set up" (Heb. 8.2). He "presentifies" — to coin an awkward term in order to make clear the real meaning of the word "re-presents" — the one who is *always* present mystically by his Spirit and in his Body (Heb. 10.15-16). The liturgical tradition of the Eastern Church states clearly that Christ himself is the unique High Priest and sole celebrant of every liturgy, and the particular *proestōs,* or leader, functions to make him present. Thus the *Anaphora Prayer* from the *Liturgy of St. John Chrysostom* stresses that the priest administers only what was delivered *to* him from the Lord, and received *from* him by the Lord. Hence, for Eastern Christians, since the priest serves liturgically *in persona Christi,* it is Christ himself who reconciles them to the Father through the liturgical rite. He is at one and the same time "the Offered and the Offerer." However distinctive this emphasis may be in the East, the truth it conveys is common to all Christian worship.

13. See Joseph J. Allen, "Pastoral Theology in North America," *Ecumenism* 7 (1985), 17-20, where the "modes" of ministry are developed.

A second mode in the ministry of reconciliation is the prophetic office of *teacher* or *proclaimer.* Its substance, motive, and meaning are always the same: the "Good News" — εὐαγγέλιον [*Euangelion*] about the Reconciler: "Jesus is the Lord!" Those who engage in this second mode of ministry are bound like the Apostle: "I handed on to you as of first importance what I in turn had received" (1 Cor. 15.3). The "Ministry of the Word" (Διακονία τοῦ Λόγου [*Diakonia tou Logou*] must always be consistent with the Gospel delivered to the apostolic Church: "Whether then it were I or they, so we proclaim and so you have come to believe" (1 Cor. 15.11). Nevertheless, this mode is a good deal more subjective than the liturgical aspects of worship. It is truly an area of *periptōsis,* appropriation, "applied theology." The always-the-same message of reconciliation must be contextualized, applied to each particular scenario. The universal must be made specific. This is a very difficult task today, but also one of the most crucial to the success of the overall ministry of the Church.

Even more subjective, more requiring of appropriation, is the third mode of ministry: that of spiritual direction itself. Having introduced it within the broad context of providing total care to the people of God, with the specific goal of bringing them to reconciliation, the remainder of the book will be given over to exploring the various facets and concerns of the *inner way.* Our first step is to examine its history.

# 2 The Historical Tradition of the Inner Way

*Why do you increase your bonds? Take hold of your life before your light grows dark, and seeking help you do not find it. This life has been given to you for repentance; do not waste it in vain pursuits.*

St. Isaac of Syria

*Metanoia is the daughter of hope and the denial of despair.*

St. John Climacus

## 1. Eldership: Distinctions and Connections

Ivan Kontzevitch, a spiritual son of the Elder Nektary of the famous Optino Monastery in Russia, argues that in its nascent form — "eldership" — spiritual direction can be traced back to the apostolic age itself.[1] This places him somewhat at odds with the majority of writers on the subject, who see the elder emerging in the fourth century with the great flourishing of monasticism in the Middle East.[2] He bases his conviction

1. Kontzevitch, "Eldership," 35-44.

2. See Leech, *Soul Friend*, 41, where he summarizes the literature: "The first sign of spiritual direction within the Christian Tradition on any sizeable scale can be seen

on the fact that the second-century *Didachē* already bears witness to one of the prime requirements laid on practitioners of this "prophetic ministry":

> Sanctity of life, indeed, was required of the prophet from the first period of Christianity: "He must have the manner of the Lord. From his manner may be distinguished the false prophet and the [true] prophet."[3]

Kontzevitch finds further support for his claim in the fact that in St. Paul's lists of the categories of ministry in Eph. 4.11 and 1 Cor. 12.28, prophecy is included in the top three — along with apostleship and teaching — and that in 1 Cor. 14.3 his characterization of the function of prophecy — *edification, exhortation,* and *comfort* — corresponds with the functions of the elder in spiritual direction. I would differ with Kontzevitch only in maintaining that it is insignificant whether the practitioners of spiritual direction who demonstrated these three functions be labeled "elders" or something else. What is vital is that edification, exhortation, and comfort have marked this ministry *ab initio* with the Great Apostle, because they belong to the very διακονία [*diakonia:* ministry] of the Church herself in *every* age. I would not dispute, however, that spiritual direction did indeed reach great heights in the

---

in the Desert Fathers of Egypt, Syria and Palestine in the fourth and fifth centuries." See also Sebastian P. Brock, *The Syriac Fathers on Prayer and the Spiritual Life,* Cistercian Studies, 101 (Kalamazoo, MI: Cistercian Publications, 1987), especially the opening section devoted to Oriental Christianity, where monasticism is seen flourishing in what he terms the "third stream of Christian tradition" alongside the Greek and Latin. See also *Barsanuphius and John Questions and Answers (Patrologia Orientalis,* 31.3), ed. Derwas J. Chitty (Paris: Firmin-Didot, 1966). Chitty cites four distinct groups of manuscripts from Mount Athos — the *Coislianius, Vatopedi, Nikodemus,* and *Sinaiticus* — which clearly reveal the early use of "letter writing" as a form of spiritual direction by "two spiritual old men living in quiet in a coenobium in the region of Gaza" (i.e., Palestine). The *Pachomian Chronicle and Rules (Pachomian Koinonia,* 2), translated by Armand Veilleux (Kalamazoo, MI: Cistercian Publications, 1981), shows how the monastic life flourished in Egypt through the Coptic texts of Pachomius, Theodore, and Harsiesios. Finally, Waddell in *Desert Fathers* bears witness to the character of early monasticism in the Middle East from its roots in the life of St. Antony the Great recorded in the *Vita Antonii* of St. Athanasius of Alexandria.

3. Kontzevitch, "Eldership," 35, 44. He cites Prof. Konstantin Dmitrievich Popov's monumental Russian-language study of the *Didache: Uchenie dvenadtsati apostolov: nedavno otkrytoe sochinenie vremen apostolov* (Moscow: I. D. Sytin, 1898).

"science and art" of the elder — and so will turn now to this specific application.

The Eastern deserts gave birth to monasticism, an essentially "lay" vocation. The earliest elders were drawn predominantly from the ranks of the *lay monks.* In the West, early on, priestly orders per se came to be viewed as an adequate criterion for offering spiritual direction, and the context was largely reduced to the hearing of sacramental confessions and the granting of absolution. While the same situation pertained in the East, the distinction was never as radical. While hierarchs and monastics might argue over who had the right to serve as a spiritual director, the bone of contention tended to be the place of this practice within the overall structure of the Church. This was the prevailing concern, rather than the denial that the minister of repentance had to be specially qualified through the possession of divinely given spiritual gifts.[4] St. John the Faster of Constantinople writes bluntly: "Our Lord Jesus Christ has given the prophets, apostles, bishops, and priests to teach spiritual doctrine, and *monks* to receive the confessions of sinners."[5] There may have been *practical* as well as spiritual reasons for this distinction: it appears that the duties of bishops and presbyters in their public ministry were too great to allow them the time-consuming task of spiritual direction. At any rate, in the eighth and ninth centuries, during Iconoclasm, the hearing of confessions was almost exclusively the responsibility of the monks, and it is clear from shocked observations by Western Christians in the Fourth Crusade that the power of the Eastern monks over the spiritual life of the people had not died out by the thirteenth century.[6]

On the other hand, the seventh-century *Syntagma,* a compilation of rules on spiritual matters including confession, shows that the clergy were becoming involved in the process — even if the power to remit sins had to be specifically *delegated* to individual clergymen by their bishop — thus upholding the idea of a special charisma rather than an "automatic" power imparted through the rite of ordination. By the thirteenth century some in Byzantium advocated a wholesale clerical takeover of spiritual direction, and certain Greek theologians claim that by the nineteenth century the modern view had prevailed — that the

4. *Logos pros ton Mellonta Exagoreusoi ton Heautou Pneumatikon Patera* in *Patrologiae Cursus Completus. Series Graeca* 88, ed. J.-P. Migne (1920) (hereafter cited as PG).

5. *Epistolē pros tina Monachon Theodosion* in PG 100.1065ff.

6. Cited in McNeill, *History of the Cure of Souls,* 307.

sacramental aspects of confession and absolution are the proper domain of the ordained clergy. Nevertheless, McNeill argues that "the *pneumatikoi,* those of marked spiritual attainment, had become and continue to be, a permanent element in Eastern Christianity and highly important, especially in Russian piety, through the modern age."[7]

It is important to remember that spiritual direction and confession/absolution are *not* identical, even if — especially in the Eastern Churches — they have today been largely linked in a unified sacramental rite. In order to understand the nature of the *process of healing and reconciliation,* we must continue to examine the nonsacramental component.

## 2. The Work and the Fruit: Nonsacramental and Sacramental

The *inner way* requires both spiritual direction and sacramental confession/absolution. If the former is to be successfully reawakened today,

7. *Ibid.,* 308-9. See also Leech, *Soul Friend,* 41, who states: "By the fourth century, the term *pneumatikos pater* was well established in patristic writing."

Various sources point to a seemingly radical view held by the great 14th-century mystic, St. Symeon the New Theologian: Joost Van Rossum, "Priesthood and Confession in St. Symeon the New Theologian," *St. Vladimir's Theological Quarterly* 20.4 (1976), 220-28; John Meyendorff, *The Byzantine Legacy in the Orthodox Church* (Crestwood, NY: St. Vladimir's Seminary Press, 1982); and Abp. Basil Krivochein, *St. Simeon the New Theologian* (Crestwood, NY: St. Vladimir's Seminary Press, 1986) — particularly Chapter 6; and Chapter 5 of Fr. Meyendorff's *Byzantine Theology* (New York: Fordham University Press, 1976). Our purpose here is not to examine the "charismatic and personal" theology of St. Symeon per se, but merely to point to his approach toward the observable transfer of the power and privilege to "bind and loose" in absolution from the ordained clergy to the monks as "the elected people of God": "It was not taken away from the bishops and the priests, but rather they deprived themselves of it" (Van Rossum). Fr. Meyendorff writes that Symeon "fought for the right of non-ordained monks to exercise spiritual direction *and to hear confession*" (*Byzantine Legacy,* 212). Furthermore, "he does not distinguish clearly between spiritual counsel or 'healing,' and the sacramental act of binding and loosing" (Van Rossum), not because of any "revolutionary and sectarian" tendencies, nor any desire to form an "ideal church of mystics." Rather, his anti-hierarchical texts resulted from a prophetic-like reaction against the "worldliness and secularization" which marked the clergy of his day. One must recognize that this charismatic approach, however warranted, could endanger the structures of a sound ecclesiology.

the relationship between the two must be clarified. We can begin to see the dynamic only after we have understood the proper meaning of the word "repentance." Bishop Kallistos Ware observes that it is normally taken to mean

> sorrow for sin, a feeling of guilt, a sense of grief . . . at the wounds we have inflicted on others and ourselves. Yet such a view is incomplete . . . this is not the whole of it, nor even the most important part. We come closer to the heart of the matter if we reflect on the literal sense of the Greek term for repentance, *metanoia.* This means "change of mind": and not just regret for the past, but a fundamental *transformation of our outlook, a new way of looking at ourselves, at others, and at God.* In the words of the *Shepherd of Hermas,* it is "a great understanding."[8]

Properly understood, μετάνοια [*metanoia*] means something far deeper and more radical than change at the cognitive or intellectual level. It requires that one's entire being be changed, and it begins with one's interior perspective. It is more akin to "transformation of life" or "change of heart." An "interior dynamic" is required — a change *from* something *to* something else. Sorrow and grief are necessary prerequisites to change, and open the door to "a new way of looking at oneself, others, and God." But the *to something* is as important, for it introduces that positive note of hope and healing needed to transport the directee beyond the sorrow and grief of his or her *from,* to a life filled with the potential of God's grace. Furthermore, this view of repentance binds together the *work* done in spiritual direction and the *fruits* which one reaps from re-entrance into the Body of Christ through sacramental confession/absolution.

History shows that *functionally* the ministries of elder and confessor are not identical.[9] Spiritual direction functions as a form of "guidance," ideally performed in a series of engagements, dialogues, and explorations between spiritual director and directee. Although direction has probably always played some part in the sacramental phase of healing, one must question whether the sacramental setting is *ideal* for it. Put another way, we might ask whether the fruits can be received without the work first being done.

8. "The Orthodox Experience of Repentance," *Sobornost* 1.2 (1980), 19.

9. Bp. Kallistos Ware, "The Spiritual Father in Orthodox Christianity," *Cross Currents* (Summer/Fall 1974), 297.

The work need not depend on the institutional expression of the Church. Bishop Kallistos writes that "while the confessor must always be a priest [clergy], the *starets* may be a monk not in holy orders, or a nun, a layman or a laywoman, since his or her function is essentially charismatic and prophetic: the *starets* gives advice, not only at Confession, but on many other occasions."[10] Kontzevitch expands upon this theme:

> It is a special kind of sanctity, and therefore may inhere in *anyone.* A monk without rank, but also a bishop . . . a priest. . . . Finally, Eldership can also be taken on by a *woman,* as for example, the Blessed Paraskeva Ivanovna, a fool-for-Christ in the Diveyevo Convent without whose advice nothing was ever undertaken in that monastic community.[11]

Adds Ware, the elder "is the expression of the Church as 'event' or 'happening,' rather than the Church as institution."[12] Of course, the institutional and charismatic/prophetic should never be radically opposed; within the one Church they explain one another, indeed grow out of each other, within her single ministry of healing. Tradition *does* indicate, however, that the ministry of eldership is far deeper in function than what can be encompassed in the sacrament of confession/absolution, for "only a very few confessor priests would claim to speak with the former's insight and authority."[13]

From this broad understanding of repentance, we can see that spiritual direction has always depended on a proper "disclosure of thought." Thoughts — λογισμοί [*logismoi*] in the classic vocabulary — designated not merely the mental activities which we associate with the English word, but "images, sensible phantasms, which, when dwelt upon, make one draw toward that object existing *outside* the individual."[14] These outside provocations were termed προβολή [*probolē*]. The "work" of repentance — best done in the context of spiritual direction — was literally to fight these multitudes and force them out of

10. *Ibid.*

11. Kontzevitch, "Eldership," 40.

12. Ware, "Spiritual Father," 297.

13. *Ibid.*

14. George Maloney, "The Elder of the Christian East as Spiritual Healer," in *Studies in Formative Spirituality* (1982), 83.

one's life through disclosure. This was the way to gain one's freedom from the terrible state of "pre-conditioning" or "pre-possession" which manifests itself in πρόλυψις [*prolypsis:* "force of habit"], that residue of memory which can strike anyone to a certain degree. Such *prolepses* interfere with a person's ability to interpret new phenomena in his or her life without reference to past patterns — thus rendering him or her impulsively prejudiced. Furthermore, they may also grow into continual phantasies and fixations of various sorts, and if so, they can become so pervasive that they begin to shape the person's entire perception and behavior. Once a person reaches this state, he or she can easily be led into πλάνη [*planē:* "delusion" or "illusion"]. Only intensive and time-consuming work over and above the sacrament of confession/absolution could help heal those who have regressed this far. As André Louf argues:

> One of the aims of the unveiling of thoughts *(logismoi)* is the bringing to the surface of tendencies lurking deep in the heart where they cause havoc because they are not shared with anybody. Brought to light they often vanish. This is, therefore, *not* a *confession of faults* which might have been committed. It is no use to ask about a known weakness: Does he who knows he is losing his soul need to inquire? Hidden thoughts (προσβολή [*prosbolē*]) are to be questioned, and it is the Elder's task to "test" them. As for visible flaws, there is no need to inquire, but simply to remove them right away.[15]

True *metanoia,* then, encompasses more than a sacramental confession of sins. It also speaks of "those ideas and impulses which may seem innocent to him [the directee], but in which the spiritual father may discern secret dangers and significant signs."[16] It is worth noting that the disclosure of thoughts in confession is essentially *retrospective;* it deals with sins that have already occurred. Spiritual direction, by contrast, is essentially *preventative,* even *teleological* — aimed at future spiritual development — by disclosing those *logismoi* which might lead a person into sin if left unchecked. In this first phase of healing, that is, spiritual direction, "the purpose of this self-disclosure is not juridical,

15. André Louf, "Spiritual Fatherhood in the Literature of the Desert," in *Abba: Guides to Wholeness and Holiness, East and West,* Cistercian Studies, 38, ed. John R. Sommerfeldt (Kalamazoo, MI: Cistercian Publications, 1982), 38.

16. Ware, "Spiritual Father," 302.

to secure absolution from guilt, but self-knowledge, that each may see himself *as he truly is.*"[17] Sacramental confession can then constitute the second phase, the fruit of "absolution from guilt."

We see here a *positive* side to *metanoia.* It is no coincidence that this healing action is often described in medical terminology. In his *Shorter Rules,* St. Basil the Great draws an analogy between bodily injuries and sins; as physical maladies can be healed only if revealed to a physician trained in curing them, so too can sins be healed only by exposing them to one empowered to forgive.[18] St. Gregory of Nyssa describes a kind of "medical science" that spiritual patients must accept from those whom they seek out for healing: "Reveal courageously even the greatest of your secrets, disclose to him the mysteries of your soul, as the patient uncovers his wounds to the physician, and you will obtain cure."[19] The healing motif is also reflected in the canons of the great councils (e.g., Laodicea, 2; and 3 Constantinople, 102, which will be discussed at greater length later) in instructing the faithful how Christian spiritual "treatment" should be approached — both by those "who have manifest their medical science in spirit" and those who "have had the healing power conferred on them."[20]

It is in this sense that the work of repentance leads to the fruit of healing. St. John Climacus says plainly: "*Metanoia* is the daughter of hope and the denial of despair."[21] It leads not to ἀκηδία [*acedia:* "despondency"], but to its opposite, *eager expectation:*

> It is not self-hatred, but the affirmation of my true self as made in God's image. To repent is to look, not downward at my own shortcomings, but upward at God's love; not backward with self-reproach, but forward with trustfulness. It is to see, not what I have *failed* to be, but what by the grace of Christ I can yet *become.*[22]

If all of this be true, then spiritual direction never ends; it is a continuing process, an on-going "attitude." This would be the case even if sin were

17. Evergenitos, *Synagogē* (Athens: Mattharon, 1957), 1, 20, 168-69.

18. *Answer 229,* cited in Seraphim Papacostas, *Repentance,* 2nd ed. (Athens: Zoe, 1958), 80.

19. *Canonical Letter,* cited in Papacostas, *Repentance,* 82.

20. *Ibid.,* 83.

21. "Step Five," *The Ladder of Divine Ascent,* trans. Lazarus Moore (Boston: Holy Transfiguration Monastery, 1978), 54-66.

22. See Ware, "Orthodox Experience," 20.

not always a possibility, because within the "interior dynamic" of *metanoia* there is always room for *growth:* "what by the grace of Christ I can yet become." The work of repentance opens up a veritable panorama of one's past, present, and potential future; one can see how much room there will be for transformation from darkness to light up until one's last breath.

> The connection between repentance and the advent of great light is particularly significant. . . . So long as a room is in darkness, says Theophan the Recluse, you do not see the dirt; but when you bring a powerful light into the room, you can distinguish every speck of dust. So it is in the room of your soul.[23]

## 3. Bringing Light into Human Motivation and Behavior

The elder's *praxis,* historically, was to work toward bringing light into the motivations and behavior of his directees, and thereby rendering them open to God's grace. But the director awaited the direct invitation of the directee before taking up this role, and thereafter made himself or herself available as a special "companion," trained as he or she was in Christian compassion. St. Isaac the Syrian counsels:

> Be a companion to those who are sad at heart, with passionate prayer and heartfelt sighs, [and] support the weak and distressed with a word as far as you are able, so that the right hand upholding the universe may sustain you.[24]

But the elder was capable of serving as a special companion only because *he* first lived through the challenges of life with θεωρία [*theōria:* "inner reflection" or "contemplation"] and ἄσκησις [*askēsis:* "struggle"]. "One who speaks about virtue from the experience of his own labor brings a word to his hearers," remarks St. Isaac.[25] Continual "inner

23. *Ibid.*

24. St. Isaac of Nineveh, *On the Ascetical Life,* Discourse 2.16-17, trans. Mary Hansbury (Crestwood, NY: St. Vladimir's Seminary Press, 1989), 36. See also Kristen Ingram, "Spiritual Directors: Companions on the Way," *Ministry* (Sept. 1988), 8-10.

25. *Ibid.,* Discourse 1.32.

reflection" on his own life, which formed part of a vibrant prayer life, allowed the elder to develop the crucial capacity for διάκρισις [*diakrisis:* "discernment"]. It was this discernment which he sought to develop in others, for the more one is able to discern about life, the more light can be brought into the heart and mind.

The more one studies the history of eldership the more evident it becomes that this virtue was absolutely central — first for the elder himself, then for the directee. Why should discernment (sometimes called "discrimination" in the ascetical literature, but without the pejorative connotations now attaching to the English term) occupy such a prominent place? Why is it, indeed, the chief characteristic in the history of spiritual direction? Because this gift is the elder's key to maintaining balance and equilibrium in guiding his directees, and balance and equilibrium measure the health of one's spiritual life. St. John Cassian lauded discernment as a type of "'eye' or 'lantern' of the soul," capable of:

> teach[ing] a man to walk the royal road, swerving neither to the right through extreme self-control [i.e., extreme compulsion, fastidiousness or scrupulosity], nor to the left through indifference and laxity.[26]

This virtue allowed the elder to remain alert and vigilant, practicing a life of ρποσοχή [*prosochē:* "attentiveness"] and νῆψις [*nēpsis:* "watchfulness"]. An elder who practiced a life of this sort could not fail to gain the respect of the faithful. His inner coherence and comprehensive balance were projected onto everyone around him. His "presence" was known as the κράσις [*krasis:* "temperament of equilibrium"] which often attracted directees who found themselves precisely in a state of disequilibrium.[27] The elder's presence, however, was a direct result of the active attention he paid to the virtue of discernment.

When an elder had gained fame for his gift of discernment and attracted followers who sought his advice, how did he actually practice spiritual direction? Discernment was again the key. This is seen most clearly in those periods when the "work" of spiritual direction was differentiated from the "fruits" in confession/absolution. The director

26. In the *Philokalia,* I, ed. G. E. H. Palmer, Philip Sherrard, and Kallistos Ware (Boston: Faber & Faber, 1979), 99-100.

27. See *Philokalia* for a further explanation of these terms, which are also common to the rest of the literature of spiritual direction.

called upon his directee to "manifest" or "disclose" him- or herself in a process called ἐξαγορεύεσις [*exagoreuesis:* "telling out" or "declaration"]. In fact communal monasticism incorporated a daily "opening of the soul" by each monk, either to the abbot or to a companion designated to serve as his father confessor.

The director initially works to push the directee "back on himself," bringing him to face his inner being, to see what is there, what is operating, what is true. To travel the *inner way* means to allow the light of discernment, about which St. John Cassian spoke, to probe the depths of one's heart and mind. The elder's function is to guide the person into the places where such discoveries can be made because light has newly shined upon them. And what does he hope the directee will see? Again, both his *motivation* (perception) and his *behavior,* which together constitute a person's life.

Thus, if a directee's *behavior* proves to be an act of revenge, his *motivation* could well be envy or hatred; if his behavior includes an act of harsh judgment against another, the motivation might well be arrogance or haughtiness. The literature of Eastern Christianity, such as the *Philokalia* and *Apophthegmata Patrum,* demonstrates that the elders used the virtue of discernment to lead their charges toward a deeper understanding of the hidden operations in their lives. They spoke of this simply as bringing the light of truth into the inner person. If such light shines in the darker recesses of a directee's life, it enables him or her to begin the struggle which leads into deeper communion with God.

The elders used simple terms because they did not share the modern taste for diagnostic, clinical labels. Nevertheless, we see them performing in their spiritual direction healing techniques which science has since "proven" beneficial in restoring people to wholeness and mental health. When possible, the elder would seek to connect motivations to behaviors. When this was impossible, it was either because the elder discerned that the directee could not bear delving this deeply, or would be incapable of gaining any healing benefit from such an exploration. Still, some healing was realized at the purely behavioral level.

The most critical step in the process of healing was the directee's willingness freely to enter the *inner way.* The initiative had always to be taken by him or her — never the elder: otherwise the facades would never have dropped. Such "surrendering" was, and is, painful. It is akin to spiritual death, but it is the only way in which the healing process can begin. "Who loses his life will save it," says the Lord (Mt. 10.39), and the paradox of these words will never end: only in letting go does one receive; only in surrendering the old can the new be born.

The elder knew that the directee would have to recognize and struggle with the variety of obstacles which blocked his spiritual growth. As he put into practice the first step of healing — the work of *metanoia* — he stressed the Eastern Christian teaching that by virtue of the image of God with which he or she was born, it is *natural* for every person to grow toward union with God. There he is most himself, unless such growth be blocked by obstacles and sins: self-pity, resentfulness, guilt — appropriate and inappropriate — irritation, envy, anger, etc. These, when not discerned, lead to forms of behavior which cause the person to traverse an *alien* path, away from his natural being and communion with God.

Such obstacles can be overcome, but not "automatically." Led by the elder, the directee must become ever more discerning; he or she must acknowledge negative motivations and perceptions. The elder helps "educate" the directee about his or her particular interior phenomena. Healing is slowed whenever the directee succeeds in *camouflaging* interior operations, even from himself. A multitude of devices and masks are used: denial, avoidance, blaming others, compensation, projection onto others, etc. The common denominator to them all is that they prevent a person from seeing any evil intent in his or her own actions. They are at best lies, and can easily develop into "idols" capable of holding the person in virtual bondage. The elders may not have used the modern clinical labels for these defense mechanisms, but they certainly were aware of their use by directees intent on avoiding the truth — which is the only thing that can set us free (Jn. 8.32). The *inner way* points to this unity of light with truth.

The role of discernment in spiritual direction has profound *moral* as well as *psychological* implications. When an elder agreed to direct a person, he did those things necessary to increase both the person's consciousness and his or her ethical decision-making. Both are necessary, for the Christian's aim must be a life of ἀρετή [*aretē:* "virtue"]. Early on in his *praxis* of direction, the elder would attempt to elevate the directee's *consciousness* regarding motivations and behavior. This is the point at which modern, secular counselors may tend to stop, content at having provided certain psychological insights. In spiritual direction, by contrast, the elevation of consciousness is meant to sharpen the directee's *conscience,* that medium which the biblical literature informs us is crucial to God's ability to speak to human beings.

Indeed, in spiritual direction, becoming more conscious — that is, more psychologically aware — is not of value in and of itself; "increased consciousness" is not our ultimate goal. Rather, it is a necessary "pivot," taking the person *beyond* him- or herself.[28] By elevating a directee's consciousness, one hopes to see him or her develop a better relationship with his or her own "depths." In turn, one's depths form not only a "receptacle" for the many negative and dark components as is so often held by secular therapies, but also the abode of sources of light and healing. In these depths reside not just a kind of "experience," or even just increased "insights" as an end-point, but rather the presence of God himself, whose healing hand of grace can touch those elements which emerge through one's increased consciousness.

The literature on spiritual direction clearly indicates that the elder's gift of discernment was used to heighten both consciousness and conscience. His *praxis* united awareness (which in modern jargon is a *psychological* principle) and conscience (which is an *ethical* principle). That the two are, in fact, profoundly related is shown by the existence of but one Greek term to cover both: συνείδησις [*syneidesis*].[29] If one's consciousness of right and wrong is not raised, his conscience — as moral judge — cannot function properly. One can hardly approach God in a truthful manner if one's conscience is asleep. When the conscience sleeps one cannot find that true knowledge which is discovered as one treads the *inner way.*

## 4. The Inner Way to True Knowledge

As we explore the relationship between consciousness and conscience, we learn that the elders directed those who sought their help toward what the Eastern Christian tradition calls "true knowledge" or better φυσικὴ γνώσις [*physikē gnōsis:* "natural knowledge"]. The discovery —

28. See Louis Bouyer, *Introduction to Spirituality* (London: Darton, Longman and Todd, 1963), 17-23. The author shows both the connections and the limitations of consciousness in spiritual growth.

29. *Ibid.* See also Harakas, *Toward the Transfigured Life,* 107-13, where the author explains the relationship of these various terms to the development of conscience: *syneidesis, peporomene syneidesis* ("hardened conscience"), and *diakrisis* (where one sees the relationship of consciousness and conscience).

or uncovering — of this knowledge requires the activity of both psychological and moral faculties. What *is* this "natural knowledge," then, and how do these factors figure in its acquisition?

We can understand the meaning of the phrase only by moving beyond the empirical categories which we commonly associate with secular knowledge. Discursive reasoning, sense experience, pragmatic learning, etc., all figure in our daily lives, being routinely acquired through inductive or deductive reasoning, and they are not unimportant to us. True knowledge, however, transcends them. Its acquisition demands not only "learning" but also "faith." In spiritual direction one examines one's behavior, motivations, level of discernment, level of light, etc., and learns to see inwardly. Inner sight is free of the severe limitations of external sight and knowledge. By observing one's interior thoughts, emotions, senses, habits, etc. and then *struggling* with these, one learns to cultivate that which is good and virtuous, those things which God originally intended for humankind. This, in turn, enables the person to grow into the "true" or *ultimate* knowledge which consists of the deepest possible knowledge of one's self, of reality itself, and of God himself. This awareness of divine intention lies implanted in the human being from the very beginning — within God's own image within us. It is for this reason that the elder pushed his directee toward self-observation:

> They emphasized self-observation . . . they especially listened attentively to the voice of conscience and followed its promptings. It is in this way that one advanced in self-knowledge, and through self-knowledge to a knowledge of the whole of reality. "He who knows himself knows everything," says St. Anthony the Great. Similarly, Peter Damascene says, "To him who has come to know himself is given knowledge of all things."[30]

By heeding the promptings of his or her conscience, the directee can grow toward the *inner way* and thus gain more and more true knowledge. This is true because the conscience is the place where natural knowledge dwells. This is where the elder seeks to direct his charges. One must remember, however, to distinguish between "natural knowledge" *(physikē gnōsis)* and "knowledge according to [our] nature" (κατὰ

30. Constantine Cavarnos, *Byzantine Thought and Art* (Belmont, MA: Institute for Byzantine and Modern Greek Studies, 1968), 38-39.

φύσιν γνώσις [*kata physin gnōsis*]).[31] The former, which is discovered within one's depths, is *innate* and "natural" because it is a constituent part of our human nature. It is not "learned" *as such.* On the other hand, knowledge learned according to our nature is acquired by means of external inquiry, study, and searching, and is thus subject to all the distortions of our "fallen" world.

The "voice" of our conscience must, therefore, be kept wide awake and speaking to us. If it falls asleep — is removed from the consciousness — this deadens our capacity to discover true knowledge, which always includes the presence of the divine. St. John Chrysostom utilizes another image of "deadening" to warn of dangers to the conscience:

> As in severe frost all limbs are stiffened and dead, so truly the soul shuddering in the winter of sins also performs none of its proper functions, stiffened as it were by a frost on one's conscience. For what cold is to the body, that an evil conscience is to the soul.[32]

The conscience is not merely the "negative" force of the punishing "super-ego" as in Freudian teaching, but rather an "impartial judge" which at times can prove an affirming, *positive* guide (see Rom. 2.15). According to Abba Dorotheus:

> When God created man, he implanted in him something divine, like a certain warm and luminous thought, having a spark of reason to illumine the mind and distinguish good from evil. This is called "conscience" and is "natural law."[33]

In this common teaching of the Greek fathers, we see the conscience portrayed as the voice of "natural law" within us, capable of speaking not only about what is evil and to be avoided, but also about what is good and deserving to be done. The elders were not concerned about "how the conscience is formed" — which would probably be the focus of investigation today. Rather, believing the conscience to be a natural voice implanted by God, they urged their directees to listen to it carefully. They also took pains to help them interpret its message. The importance of the conscience as a positive moral guide is stressed by St.

31. *Ibid.,* 36.
32. *Homily VII (2 Cor. iii. 7, 8)* in NPNF 12.314.
33. *Didaskalia* 2.9 (PG 88.1652), cited in Cavarnos, *Byzantine Thought,* 41.

Maximus the Confessor: "Do not dishonor your conscience which always gives you excellent counsel, for it offers you divine and angelic advice";[34] and by St. John Climacus: "After God, let us have our conscience as our aim and rule in everything."[35]

The fathers stressed that the conscience is never truly lost or destroyed — surely a hopeful sign! It can, however, be otherwise maltreated:

> Is the conscience destroyed as a "faculty"? The answer is that the conscience is never destroyed, but only ceases to operate as a result of being continually ignored or suppressed. It becomes embedded in the subconscious level of the psyche and ceases to manifest itself at the level of consciousness. . . . Abba Dorotheos speaks of the "buried" conscience; he sees the first appearance of this state as an accompaniment of the Fall.[36]

The *Philokalia* warns that by continually "trampling on our conscience, we bury it and it is no longer able to speak to us clearly." Dorotheus in like manner explains that as it fades and grows dimmer, "we do not apprehend what our conscience tells us, and we almost think that we do not have it. But there is no one who does not have it, and it is never lost."[37] In our own day, Constantine Cavarnos reflects: "We are confronted with the problem of how conscience may be brought increasingly into our consciousness, so that its voice can be heard with more and more clarity."[38] This has always been, of course, the central task of spiritual direction; Abba Dorotheus guided his followers to resist the dangerous habit of disregarding their natural voice within, "for it is in this way that one runs the risk of falling into complete unconsciousness *(anaisthēsia).*"[39]

Hence, in being led on the *inner way,* one's task is precisely to bring the conscience into greater and greater consciousness; this, in turn, constitutes the discovery of "true knowledge" through interior enlightenment:

34. *Philokalia* 1.330, cited in Cavarnos, 41.
35. *The Ladder,* 124, cited in Cavarnos, 41.
36. *Philokalia,* 1.18, cited in Cavarnos, 45.
37. Cited in Cavarnos, 46.
38. *Ibid.,* 45.
39. PG 88.1653, 1656, cited in Cavarnos, 45.

> Abba Isaiah says, "Let us not give any offense to our conscience, but observe ourselves with fear of God until our conscience frees itself and a 'union' between it and us takes place." The union *[henōsis]* spoken of here is the entrance of conscience into consciousness. Philotheos adds, "attention" distinctly purifies conscience, and conscience having been purified, like a light that has been uncovered, shines brightly, driving away a great darkness.[40]

It is in the very struggle for such a "union" that one can aspire to true knowledge of his or her own inner life, of the whole of reality, and of God himself.

When the elder offered spiritual direction, then, it was at the level of both ethics and psychology, of conscience and consciousness, and he did so whether or not he was aware of the formal "operating principles." Above all, he was intent on the directee seeing the *truth* of his or her life and everything that was operating within it. At the base of his *praxis* was the diagnostic tool of discernment. For the elder, this virtue constituted the "source, root, and head of every virtue."[41] Every other virtue was conditioned by it, such that St. John Cassian could claim, "Without the gift of discernment, no virtue can stand or remain firm to the end, for it is the mother of all virtues."[42]

As the *inner way* is traversed, then, this "mother of all virtues" forms the guide in bringing light into human motivation and behavior. Only when this light is allowed to penetrate one's depths are the conditions put in place for God's grace to bring healing to the sufferer. But even the virtue of discernment would prove ineffectual if one were not willing to *disclose* the contents of his or her heart and mind to the director in an atmosphere of mutual trust.

### 5. Self-Disclosure and Trust

It is evident that although spiritual direction was widely practiced in the Eastern Church, not everyone availed him- or herself of this opportunity to pursue the inner way — even in times and places where the

40. *Philokalia,* 1.18, cited in Cavarnos, 46.
41. St. Nilus of Ancyra, *Peri ton Okto tes Kakias Logismon* in PG 79.1468.
42. Cassian, cited in *Philokalia,* 1.100.

observance of sacramental confession/absolution was virtually universal. This despite the warning of such as St. Isaac the Syrian that "the pains of a hard heart grow, and the sick person who resists the physician increases his own suffering."[43] Or the noteworthy distinction made by Russian starets St. Macarius of Optino between the easy contentedness of those who resist spiritual direction and the hard-won peace of those who pursue the inner way:

> As to those who are happy without seeking spiritual direction, and are quite blissful without bothering much about the deeper Christian life — the life of the mind and the heart — theirs is the peace of this world, not the peace of the Master. Whenever we do set out firmly to tread the *inner way*, a storm of temptations and persecutions always assails us. It is because of the dark host that spiritual direction is profitable, nay necessary to us, whether we retire to a monastery or continue to live in the world.[44]

Why would anyone want to *avoid* treading this inner way? Why would one resist the light and the healing that it brings? There are a multitude of reasons, but they share a common root: the fear of the pain which is inherent in the healing process. St. John of the Ladder points to the foremost cause of resistance: *self-reliance:*

> Those who rely on themselves and think that they have no need for any guide are deceiving themselves. . . . Without a guide, one wanders from the road, however prudent one may be.[45]

Self-reliance prevents the enlightenment necessary for the fullness of healing to occur. This fullness only *begins* to be attained in a relationship of trust with an elder, as one discloses oneself in the dialogical encounter.

As we have noted, the elder attempted in the best of circumstances to lead his directees to see both *what* they were doing (behavior) and *why* they were doing it (perception/motivation). This painful process of self-scrutiny is the work of repentance proper, and is performed as the first phase of the healing process. Later, when this "work" was

43. *On the Ascetical Life,* Second disourse, 32.

44. *Russian Letters of Direction, 1834-1860,* trans. by Iulia de Beausobre (Crestwood, NY: St. Vladimir's Seminary Press, 1975), 28.

45. *Ladder,* Steps 1.7 and 26.37, pp. 5 and 167, respectively.

completed, the elder could send the directee to the clergy for sacramental confession/absolution, the second and final phase of healing. But the whole process was forestalled if one relied upon him- or herself — "however prudent one may be."

Only when one realizes what takes place in the two phases of healing is it possible to grasp the true meaning of the sacrament of confession/absolution as the wonderful *fruit* of repentance. In short, when the initial atmosphere of trust is present — and this is always the opposite of self-reliance — the *work* of spiritual direction can lead us to the *fruit* of the sacrament.

In the Eastern Christian tradition, the sacrament of confession/absolution is best understood as an εἴσοδος [*eisodos:* "entrance" — or better, "re-entrance"] into the communion of the Church. In fact, St. John Climacus describes this sacrament as an "initiation," boldly calling it the "baptism of tears":

> The baptism of tears after Baptism is greater than Baptism itself, although this may seem strange to say. . . . Our first Baptism we received as infants, but we have polluted it; through tears we regain the purity of our first Baptism.[46]

The weeping sinner has, however, to be led to understand that this re-entrance can occur only as a result of his or her own ἄσκησις [*askēsis:* "struggle"] and work. That this is the necessary prerequisite is captured in a story in the *Apophthegmata Patrum,* in which a monk begged St. Anthony of Egypt to pray for him. Anthony replied, "Neither will I take pity on you, nor will God himself, unless you make some effort on your own."[47] One's own effort is the beginning of the process. God's blessing comes at the end.

However, if the healing process is to begin at all, it will take what St. John Climacus demands: the abandonment of self-reliance. He and other fathers asked, How can a person truly be led to *metanoia* — "changing of the mind" — while relying on him- or herself? How can he or she reach the first phase of healing, the θεραπεία Θεοῦ [*therapeia Theou:* "therapy of God"] without entering a humble relationship with a trusted other (e.g., an elder, spiritual friend, etc.)?

46. *Ibid.,* Step 7, pp. 70-88.

47. *The Desert Christian: Sayings of the Desert Fathers: The Alphabetic Collection,* trans. Benedicta Ward (New York: Macmillan, 1979).

As we have said, this is not to deny the fundamental doctrine that God is free to do as he wishes, but healing seems to occur most readily through such a relationship of openness and trust between a spiritual director and a directee practicing ἐξαγορεύεσις [*exagoreuesis:* "disclosure"]. As St. Isaac the Syrian observes: "The sick one who is familiar with his illness is easily cured, and the one who acknowledges his pain is close to healing."[48] But how is one to reach such realization of one's condition without abandoning pride and self-reliance? These will always block the spirit of disclosure and trust.

Here we must emphasize that, especially according to the Eastern tradition, to accomplish one phase of the healing process without moving on to the next is to "short-circuit" the entire process. To enter a trusting dialogue with a director and do the "work" of repentance without looking beyond this to sacramental absolution, and thus the possibility of eucharistic communion, offers little more than the psychological discovery one could get from secular practitioners. In true spiritual direction, "insight" is never enough; one can possess psychological insights into one's perceptions and motivations and yet never *change* one's actions. Insight is but a necessary beginning point.

The opposite, however, is also true. If no work and struggle precedes our approaching confession/absolution, we risk reducing the sacramental act to a "magical lifting" of sins. Such an approach — void of active repentance and any *real* contrition — becomes a highly antiseptic way of dealing with the reality of sin, one which mystifies the reality of forgiveness by reducing it to a mere reward for correctly practicing the prescribed rituals. This, in turn, robs the liturgical form of any real content.

It is important to remember here that the initiator of the relationship of trust and disclosure should always be the directee, for by taking the initiative to enter a dialogue, he or she affirms his or her trust in the elder. St. Ignatius Brianchaninov forbids giving advice of one's own accord, before a person *asks* for it:

> The voluntary giving of advice is a sign that we regard ourselves as possessed of spiritual knowledge and worth, which is a clear sign of pride and self deception.[49]

48. St. Isaac, *On the Ascetical Life,* Second disourse.

49. *The Arena: An Offering to Contemporary Monasticism,* trans. Lazarus Moore (Madras, India: Diocesan Press, 1970), 49.

To which St. Macarius of Optino adds, "I cannot possibly give her any guidance unless she herself *asks* for it.[50]

The relationship of trust itself, initiated by the directee and responded to by the elder, provides the proper environment for self-disclosure. Kenneth Leech stresses the importance of this relationship:

> In early Christianity, reference to personal relationship with a priest is sometimes related specifically to the need for penance and restoration to . . . the Christian community. . . . Thus St. Basil (330-379) tells his readers to find a man "who may serve you as a sure guide in the work of leading a holy life," one who knows "the straight road to God," and he warns that "to believe that one does not need counsel is great pride."[51]

According to the *Philokalia*, when an atmosphere of trust prevails, the burden of self-disclosure is made light:

> Most importantly, in everything you do, ask to be advised by your spiritual father in Jesus Christ; for in this manner, by the grace of Christ, the unbearable and arduous become easy, and it will seem to you that you are rapidly moving along a gently sloping field.[52]

History often overlooks the fact that the need for self-disclosure to another is not limited to laypersons but applies to everyone — even the holiest of elders. As Thomas Merton writes, "The most dangerous man in the world is the contemplative that is guided by nobody. He trusts his own visions. He obeys the attractions of an interior voice but will not listen to other men."[53] If such advice is applicable to contemplative monks, however, how much more must it apply to the laity? "The influence of eldership extended far beyond the boundaries of a monastery's walls. Elders spiritually guided not only monks but also laymen."[54]

No one should ever fear disclosing him- or herself fully to an elder who is already familiar with the difficulties along "the way," and already "knows the route." Bishop Kallistos writes:

50. St. Macarius, *Russian Letters,* 27.

51. Leech, *Soul Friend,* 41.

52. *Philokalia* 5.355. See also Kontzevitch, "Eldership," 36.

53. Thomas Merton, *Seeds of Contemplation* (Norfolk, CT: New Directions, 1949), 118.

54. Kontzevitch, "Eldership," 36.

> One who climbs a mountain for the first time needs to follow a known route, and he needs with him, as a companion and guide, someone who has been up before and is familiar with the way.[55]

To which Merton adds:

> The reason for this is not only that the beginner is inexperienced and needs to be instructed and helped. Everywhere in the "sayings of the fathers" we find men who are *themselves* experienced and yet still follow the guidance of others, not trusting their own judgement.[56]

Self-disclosure and trust in spiritual direction depend, then, on the relationship engendered by the elder. His character, marked by the virtues of wisdom, humility, and love — each conditioned by his use capacity for discernment — creates the arena for self-disclosure by the directee. Such virtues — and not just chronological age — are the prerequisites for eldership! The literature clearly acknowledges that while accumulated years may seem to be a major factor in achieving experiential knowledge, one can be aged and yet not wise, humble, or loving — and such a person can never be a true "elder." St. John Cassian issues a clear warning:

> It is beneficial to reveal one's thoughts to the fathers, not just to any father, but to the spiritual elders esteemed *not because of their venerable age and gray hair,* but because of their discernment. Many men, carried away by the obvious old age of an elder, confessed their thoughts to him, but instead of being healed, they suffer harm, caused by the incompetence of their confessor.[57]

St. Ephraim the Syrian warns: "If you are not yet in a great measure inflamed with the Holy Spirit, do not aspire to hear another man's thoughts."[58] More recently, André Louf has observed: "Elder is a biblical term which implies *not age,* but rather a ministry of *wisdom* at the center of any Christian community."[59] It was to just such a man that St. Basil

55. Ware, "Spiritual Father," 296.

56. Thomas Merton, "The Spiritual Father in the Desert Tradition," in *Contemplation in a World of Action* (New York: Doubleday, 1977), 284.

57. Kontzevitch, "Eldership," 37, citing St. Ignatius Brianchaninov's *Works,* 1.545.

58. *Ibid.,* 37.

59. Louf, "Spiritual Fatherhood," 38.

the Great directed his flock, admonishing them to "find a man who can serve you as a very sure guide in the work of leading a holy life."[60]

Wisdom, humility, and love must be "burned" into the heart of an elder, not by intellectual learning and academic pursuits, but by a fervent prayer life and an experience of life which will prevent naïve judgments; he must know that "smoke and sin [are] abiding within himself, along with grace."[61] Kontzevitch warns that

> an ascetic who has, without particular effort received the gift of grace because of the purity of his soul, which he has preserved since childhood, may not have the ability to guide others. Because he is not familiar with the ways of evil from his own experience, he does not know of the warfare against passions, and therefore he does not perceive evil in others.[62]

That is, "only a man who has successfully traversed the path of spiritual labor himself, can lead others along this path." Others — even if they are truly "holy" — can cause harm to their disciples and even "drive them into delusion [πλάνη — *planē*]."[63]

Once relationship with an elder is established, dialogue can take place not only orally but through the written word. Even a cursory study of the fathers will confirm that very often direction was requested and given through letters; St. John Chrysostom, St. Basil, and St. Augustine are but three examples. The elders also utilized this method; letters poured in and out of Palestine and Egypt and later such Russian centers of direction as Optino. The testimony of St. Dorotheus of Gaza is representative:

> I was free of any sorrows, of any anxieties. If some disquieting thought occurred to me, I would write it down on a tablet, because I was used to *writing down my questions before attending to my Elder;* and no sooner would I finish writing than I would feel benefit and relief, so great was the carefreeness and peace in me.[64]

60. See Reginald Garrigou-Lagrange, *The Three Ages of the Interior Life: Prelude of Eternal Life,* vol. 1, trans. Sister M. Timothea Doyle (St. Louis: Herder, 1957-59), 256.

61. *Homilies of Macarios of Egypt,* 26.25.205.

62. Kontzevitch, "Eldership," 38, citing Metr. Philaret of Moscow's *Instructions on Fear in Christian Reading,* no. 244 (St. Petersburg, 1882).

63. Cited in Kontzevitch, 38.

64. *Ibid.*

By recording one's life experiences over a period of days or weeks, and taking this "diary" to the next dialogue with one's spiritual director, one provides the opportunity to observe patterns of behavior and motivation *over time* rather than through what can be recalled at an isolated moment. Disclosure can be fuller.

Any advice given and received in written form must be understood to pertain to that particular director and directee in that particular circumstance — something which we take for granted in "impromptu" verbal exchanges. St. Macarius of Optino commented on the necessary conditions of a written exchange:

> What I write to you, I write to you *alone,* and I must ask you to refrain from passing it on to others as a general rule of conduct for all. It is nothing of the kind. My advice to you is fashioned according to your inner and outer circumstances. Hence it can only be right for you.[65]

A similar warning was issued centuries earlier by an anonymous Syriac father:

> What nursing mother who has many children, some thirty years old, others only thirty days old, is able to set before them all one and the same food? If she were to set before them just solid food alone, then her thirty day old child would die, whereas the thirty year old would grow.[66]

A fellow Syrian adds: "Do not impose a labor beyond one's strength; otherwise you will enslave yourself to the need to please others.[67]

St. Macarius of Optino in nineteenth-century Russia, like so many of the ancient fathers and elders, made effective use of writing in offering spiritual direction. Yet his letters were always a response to *specific* initiatives taken by directees. Sometimes these epistles were brutally honest about his own limitations:

> I am very much to blame for having offended you with my unwise letter. You are right, I was indeed at my wits' end, torn between visitors, my work, my immense correspondence. Besides, I was feeling so ill,

65. St. Macarius, *Russian Letters,* 25.
66. *Book of the Steps,* 1, cited in Brock, *Syriac Fathers,* 50.
67. *Ibid.,* 87.

> so weak, that I could not find in my empty and shallow mind suitable answers to all the problems that came pouring in.[68]

Towards the end of his lamentation, St. Macarius offers a glimpse of his actual *praxis* of direction by correspondence: "In order to make things a little easier, perhaps you could *underline* the questions, thus singling them out from the rest of your text."[69]

Whether orally or in writing, self-disclosure given in trust is the key to the spiritual physician's ability to "penetrate the depths . . . in order to diagnose and find the method of healing." Kontzevitch summarizes:

> An Elder who has gained personal experience in the school of sobriety and mental prayer, who has thus mastered spiritual and psychological laws . . . must be able to penetrate the very depths of the human soul, to see the very inception of evil within it, along with the causes of the inception, in order to diagnose a disease and find the precise method of healing it.[70]

### 6. Paternity: Obedience and Freedom

At the point where the atmosphere between a spiritual director and his directee attains complete trust, thus allowing candid self-disclosure, their relationship begins to transcend mere dialogue and friendship. It is only when the relationship attains true and intimate *communion* that healing begins to take place. Such communion requires certain understandings and attitudes on *both* parts.

Most crucial is the manner in which the directee understands *obedience* and *free will.* Kenneth Leech provides a lead from history: "The spiritual director was not someone who taught a spiritual technique, but he was a father who helped to shape the inner life of his sons through prayer, concern, and pastoral care." To this observation he quickly adds, "the Eastern monks emphasized the dangers of travelling

68. St. Macarius, *Russian Letters,* 28.
69. *Ibid.*
70. Kontzevitch, "Eldership," 39.

without a guide, but there is no notion of blind obedience or domination."[71]

Obedience is most assuredly stressed in the tradition, sometimes radically so: but the demand for obedience is always intended to break down the directee's stubborn self-will and ego-pride. One of the strongest proponents of obedience is St. Symeon the New Theologian:

> Brother, constantly call upon God, that he may show you a man who is able to direct you well, one whom you ought to obey as though he were God himself, whose instructions you must carry out without hesitation, even if what he enjoins upon you appears to be repugnant and harmful. . . . It is better for you . . . than to live by your own will.[72]

He goes so far as to suggest that even if one were to see his spiritual father eating with "harlots and publicans and sinners," he should doubt his own eyes. For "eyes too make mistakes, as I have learned by experience."[73] Thus we are taught that along with obedience we are to practice νεκρώσις [*nekrōsis:* "mortification"] of our will.

Such comments should not be mistaken to mean that the person who follows this advice is left "empty" through mortification. Nor should it be thought that self-denial removes all desire and passion. Indeed, Christian ἀπάθεια [*apatheia:* "passionlessness"] has never been understood as a version of "feelingless Stoicism." St. Macarius of Optino explains:

> When our desires, illumined by our own intelligence, are aimed at bringing about good — that is, the will of God on earth — and when we act in accordance with this aim, God is well pleased and supports us.[74]

While it is true that some ascetics came close to defining *apatheia* in a manner consistent with Stoicism, the tradition as a whole radically contested such a view. *Apatheia* in a Christian context requires a meaning

71. Leech, *Soul Friend,* 41.

72. St. Symeon the New Theologian, *The Discourses,* Classics of Western Spirituality, trans. Carmino J. Decantazaro (New York: Paulist Press, 1980), 232. All subsequent references are to this edition.

73. *Ibid.,* 233.

74. St. Macarius, *Russian Letters,* 38.

> significantly different from that which it has in Stoicism. For the Stoics it means the absence of all emotions, whereas for the Byzantines it means the absence not of all emotions, but only of the wrong emotions.[75]

Thus, if an elder sought to move his directee in the path of *apatheia,* it was only to lead him or her away from attachment to things of "this world" — not only material possessions, but also such negative forces as malice, evil passions, etc. "More widely, *apatheia* means freedom from all sin and vice."[76] The final object of one's will when called to *apatheia* is the highest virtue: spiritual love. "It is significant that in St. John Climacus's *Ladder of Divine Ascent,*" Constantine Cavarnos observes, "the 29th step is 'passionlessness,' while the next one, the last, is 'faith, hope and love.' "[77]

Even if one were to fight against God's will, St. Macarius of Optino adds, "God refrains from breaking our will." If he permits us to act wrongly, it nevertheless remains *our* free will. The elder here expresses a distinctly Christian understanding of *apatheia:* it does not mean carelessness or laxity of feeling, as we might interpret the English derivative "apathy." Indeed, certain kinds of "desire" are appropriate to the Christian:

> it is nonsense to say that all desire is sinful, that we should never ask God to fulfill our wishes, that we should feebly abandon ourselves to what comes along. . . . Desire is not a sin; only the desire of evil is wrong.[78]

Such an observation has important implications for spiritual direction. When we accept the direction of an elder, we do not empty our will and *leave* it empty; rather, we do so in order for God's will to fill the "space" which before was occupied by our self-will and ego-centeredness, that is, before they were toppled from their heights. St. Symeon the New Theologian explains that it is this exchange which can even lead us to "recognize" God:

75. Cavarnos, *Byzantine Thought,* 27.

76. *Ibid.*

77. *Ibid.*

78. St. Macarius, *Russian Letters,* 38.

When the mortal attitude is eliminated by the immortal mind, then it recognizes God who has raised it.[79]

Obedience to a spiritual director is like the trusting obedience of a son or daughter to his or her own parent: hence the traditional terminology — "Abba" and "Imma." In one's relationship with father or mother, one learns "by example" more than "by words"; such is the lesson of a story in the *Apophthegmata Patrum:*

> A brother asked Abba Poemen, "Some brothers live with me: do you want me to be in charge of them?" The old man said to him, "No, just work first and foremost, and if they *live* like you, they will see to it themselves." The brother said to him, "But it is they themselves, father, who want me to be in charge of them." The old man said to him, "No, be their *example* not their legislator."[80]

When we enter a trusting relationship in order to learn by example rather than by legislation, our education is not dependent on "book learning" — even if our father or mother is highly literate and well trained. St. Isaac the Syrian counsels:

> Confide your thoughts to a man who, though lacking in learning, has studied the work in practice. Therefore, follow the advice of a man who has himself experienced all, and knows how to judge patiently what needs discrimination in your case, and can point out what is useful for you.[81]

Such an attitude will enable a directee to move beyond viewing his or her elder merely as a "teacher" or "guide" — even though teaching and guidance may well be part of his *praxis.* A truly deep relationship cannot be encompassed by such titles; it has to grow into an acknowledgment of *paternity,* as one is led as a son or daughter toward spiritual growth, toward flourishing in that potential which was granted in baptism.

The spiritual father exercised a genuine *paternity* in the name of God,

79. *The Discourses,* 296.

80. *Desert Christian,* 160.

81. St. Isaac of Syria in *Early Fathers from the Philokalia,* trans. E. Kadloubovsky and G. E. H. Palmer (Boston: Faber & Faber, 1978), 263.

> engendering the life of the Spirit in the disciple. . . . The Holy Spirit is given in Baptism. However, we know all too well, the seeds of the spiritual life planted in Baptism too often remain dormant or die altogether. The Abba or "spiritual father" was one who was recognized as a life-giving influence, under whose care these mysterious seeds would truly grow and flourish. The fathers attracted disciples who came not only for lectures and counsel, but seeking life and growth in a special relationship of *filial* love.[82]

While teaching and guiding, a spiritual parent also transmits the deepest lessons of life out of his or her own life experiences, and is thus able to heal and teach the "art of virtue" simultaneously. To this end, St. Athanasius of Sinai says that those who follow this way should "find a spiritual man, experienced and able to heal us," and emphasizes that these should possess "experience of souls."[83] St. Gregory of Sinai adds, "It is impossible for anyone to learn by himself the 'art of virtue.' "[84] It must be modelled and tutored by one's spiritual parent.

When put into *practice* this art is known as πρακτική [*praktikē*] and engages the *whole* person — motivation and behavior. Indeed, *praktikē* involves everything we have covered thus far: interior struggle, bringing light through discernment, consciousness and the conscience, trust and self-disclosure, etc. It is, however, active rather than static, a process rather than a state.

Growth toward God *never ends.* In the whole of our human life we are called to grow into "God-likeness"; we are to become like God, to struggle toward the ultimate objective of all human endeavor in θέωσις [*theosis:* "deification" or "divinization"]. This is, of course, a very lofty goal for a process rooted in everyday motivations and behavior and dealing with the passions of one's normal life!

The concept of *theosis,* so characteristic of the Eastern tradition, frames the *positive* character of spiritual direction. The process is never ending precisely because God himself can never be exhausted. There is always "more" to him, always another point of growth, another plateau to be reached. Thus spiritual direction, likewise, can never end, because even if we did not sin and fall short, even if we overcame every "block" and obstacle, even if we became as perfect as a human being can become

82. Merton, *Spiritual Direction and Meditation,* 289.
83. McNeill, *History of the Cure of Souls,* 307.
84. Cited in Leech, *Soul Friend,* 45.

— God would still be greater, and our task of becoming like him would remain. *Theosis* teaches the valuable lesson that growth is always possible.

And tradition concurs that continuous growth best occurs within an intimate relationship of paternity. The monks Callistus and Ignatius thus urge every directee to "spare no effort in trying to find a teacher and guide . . . a man bearing the spirit within him . . . humble in thought of himself, of good disposition in everything." They advise that one should,

> having found such a man, cling to him with body and spirit as a devoted son to his father and from then onwards obey all his commands implicitly, accord with him in everything, and see him not as a mere man, but as Christ himself

and conclude that one cannot hope to do this "without a guide, pondering to himself and obeying his own self-will."[85]

The spiritual director, in turn, is bound to transmit not *himself* or his own ego, but his abiding rootedness in the life of the Spirit. He transmits his example to the directee, not by spoken word alone, nor by activities alone, but by what one can only call a process of "spiritual osmosis." Indeed, his influence is much more pervasive than can be overtly observed in either actions taken or words spoken. Thus Irénèe Hausherr writes:

> The spiritual father must have the Christian perfection he would pass on to the son; his spirituality must be such that the disciple learns simply by observing and living in close contact with his father.[86]

One still might ask, Is the directee to submit to blind obedience? Is his or her free will *obliterated* by this relationship? Thomas Merton encapsulates the entire tradition:

> A more accurate expression would be "uncritical" or "unquestioning" obedience. This is not blind, unreasoning, and passive obedience of one who obeys merely in order to let himself be "broken," but the

85. *Writings from the Philokalia,* trans. E. Kadloubovsky and G. E. H. Palmer (Boston: Faber & Faber, 1961), 100, 174-75.

86. *Diréction Spirituelle et Orient Autrefois* in *Orientalia Christiana Analecta,* 144 (Rome: Pont. Institutum Orientalium Studiorum, 1955), 162.

> clear-sighted trusting obedience of one who firmly believes that his guide knows the true way to peace and purity of heart. . . . Such obedience is "blind" only in the sense that it puts aside its own limited and biased judgement; but it does so precisely because it sees that to follow one's own judgement in things one does not properly understand, is indeed to walk in darkness.[87]

Obedience does not preclude testing by a trusted guide. The *Apophthegmata Patrum* is filled with testing stories, purposely overstated and apparently excessive, designed to validate the extraordinary consequences of obedience. One tells of a certain Abba Paul who ordered his disciple John to remove the dung from the cave of a hyena. The understandably distressed disciple asked, "But what if the hyena comes after me?" To which the elder replied with a smile, "If she comes out after thee, bind her and bring her here." The beast did indeed attack that evening, but when the disciple obediently rushed forward to seize her, she fled. He pursued, calling out, "Wait, for my Abba told me to bind thee." Meanwhile, the elder grew uneasy and concerned, seeing his disciple fail to return. As the story ends, we see John "coming slowly along, and the hyena at the end of a rope behind him."[88]

Another classic story deals with Abba John the Dwarf who was ordered to plant a dry stick in the sand and to water it daily, despite the fact that he would have to travel a great distance across the desert in order to acquire the water needed. After watering the stick for three years as he was told, the monk beheld it break into fruit, which the elder promptly plucked and offered to his companions, saying "Come and taste the fruit of obedience!"[89]

How are we to understand such tales? André Louf explains them as a needed "therapy," one which only makes sense in a relationship of *paternity:*

> This apparent excess can be understood only in the light of the psychological and spiritual development it was designed to set in motion. Some borderline cases simply set up a sort of "shock therapy" that only a father can impose upon his son . . . above all because the

87. *Contemplation in a World of Action,* 289.
88. Ward, *Desert Christian,* 109.
89. *Ibid.,* 85-86.

son trusts him so totally and feels loved, without limits, without hesitation, as only God can love his children.[90]

Callistus and Ignatius in their *Directions to Hesychasts* described the same thing to their students in these terms: "First of all, choose for yourself . . . complete renunciation and perfect and sincere obedience" in order to cast out all doubt and unbelief. Then, "follow your teacher step by step as though you were a mirror; follow him as your own conscience, observing total obedience."[91] We might add that the "mirror of our conscience" provides in fact a form of "shock therapy," for who among us is *not* shocked by what he sees in himself? Obviously, the elder's aim was to deliver his followers from their false and illusory selves, and thereby to reintroduce them to the *inner way* to true freedom.

For modern readers, such stories give an impression of a total lack of free will, of the directee deprived of all power of rational judgment and choice. But if we endeavor to understand the predicament presented in these narratives, we will come to a clearer understanding of the relationship which must exist in spiritual direction.

Bishop Kallistos helps clarify the nature of Christian obedience by putting forth three principles. First, "obedience offered by the spiritual son to his Abba is not forced, but willing and voluntary." Once we decide — freely — to place ourselves under the direction of an elder, we are asked — again freely — also to surrender our own subjectivity into these trusted hands. In turn, the elder refrains from breaking our will, but rather accepts it as a gift. Submission which is forced is obviously void of moral value, so the spiritual director must wait for us to give it rather than demand it.[92] Kontzevitch concurs:

> While all members of the Church are bound to submit themselves to the Church authority, no one is bound to submit to the authority of an elder. An elder never imposes himself on anyone; one always submits to him voluntarily.[93]

Furthermore, this offering is not a one-time, unique gesture; spiritual direction calls for a *continual* offering, since it is a continuous relation-

90. Louf, "Spiritual Fatherhood," 49.
91. *Writings from the Philokalia*, 174.
92. Ware, "Spiritual Father," 306.
93. "Eldership," 40.

ship and not the reaction to an isolated life crisis. Hence, "every day and each hour, under the guidance of the Abba, the disciple will face new situations, calling for a different response, a new kind of giving."[94]

Second, "the relationship between the elder and the spiritual child is not one- but two-sided."[95] Indeed, if in this relationship the directee discovers who he is by moving beyond his own subjectivity, so too the elder must constantly discover who he is! The elder is called to be a companion and fellow sojourner; both attempt to "discern the Spirit," to listen to God, with as great docility and openness as the moment allows. St. John Climacus writes:

> Barsanuphius asked his son to pray for him that he might receive the Holy Spirit, for *He* is the "Great Pilot" . . . and it would be wrong, therefore, to reserve too much esteem for the spiritual father.[96]

Thus God is the true Spiritual Physician, and the elder merely reflects him by becoming transparent to his actions. He and the directee stand together before God. In truth the elder has no power in himself, apart from his own continuous union with God. In fact, he may not even realize the capacity that God has given him unless it is made known to him *through* his directee. "In most instances, a man does not realize that he is called to be a *starets* [elder] until others come to him and insist on placing themselves under his guidance."[97]

As the spiritual director travels with his directee along the latter's life-story, reciprocity continues between them. It is precisely this reciprocity, realized as they both stand before God, which mitigates against any "cult of personality" in spiritual direction. Louf observes:

> When a brother asked to leave monastic life because the famous Abba he sought did not take care of him, that Abba reproached him with these words: "It is just that God made me forget you, for you were depending not on him, but on me." Any cult of personality is excluded. . . . The father is useless if he is not transparent to God's actions.[98]

94. Ware, "Spiritual Father," 307.
95. *Ibid.*
96. *Ladder,* 174.
97. Ware, "Spiritual Father," 307.
98. Louf, "Spiritual Fatherhood," 59-60.

The directee will inevitably realize that his or her elder is not immune to human failure, limitations, and temptations; he has struggled with these before his spiritual child ever approached him, and must continue to do so hereafter. In fact, it is because the elder works out of his own struggles that he has no exhaustive, "pre-packaged" program to offer. On the contrary, he speaks a different word to each person he directs. And, by extension, "since the word which he gives is on the deepest level — not his own but the Holy Spirit's — he does not know in advance what that word will be."[99]

Nevertheless, he can find the "right word" for each individual, the word that will "heal" him or her, simply because their relationship is based on a union in love. Healing emerges from the communion in God which they share. Lawrence LeShan points to the mystery of this phenomenon, declaring that where a "union in love" exists, director and directee need not even be in the same room for healing to take place; indeed, there is no need even to think of healing per se.[100]

History tells us that elder and directee together proceed on their common journey, not according to some abstract rule of standard operating procedures, but according to their concrete human situation,

> neither of them knowing beforehand exactly what the outcome will be, but each waiting for the enlightenment of the Spirit. Each of them, spiritual father as well as disciple, must learn as he goes.[101]

The Syriac fathers show that director and directee must leave space for God's Spirit to act; they must remain available to him, rather than rigidly laying out a plan. John the Solitary writes:

> Do not make hard and fast decisions over anything in the future, for you are a created being and your will is subject to changes. Do decide in whatever matters you have to reach a decision, but without fixing in your mind that you will not be moved to other things. . . . Do not

99. Ware, "Spiritual Father," 307.

100. *The Medium, the Mystic, and the Physicist* (New York: Viking, 1974), 102-9. St. Seraphim of Sarov seems to point to this same phenomenon when he says, "When I am no longer with you, come to my grave and bring me all your sorrows and sufferings. Talk to me as though I were still living, for I shall always be with you" (Valentine Zander, *St. Seraphim of Sarov,* trans. Sister Gabriel Anne, S.S.C. [Crestwood, NY: St. Vladimir's Seminary Press, 1975], 112).

101. Ware, "Spiritual Father," 307.

> lay down a law for yourself, otherwise you will become a slave to these laws.[102]

In his third and final observation concerning obedience, Bishop Kallistos cautions that the elder must always avoid any form of *spiritual violence.* Should a rebuke or reproof [ἐπιτίμησις: *epitimēsis*] prove necessary, it must be delivered with "humble love," as expressed by the elder Zossima in Dostoyevsky's novel *The Brothers Karamazov:*

> At some ideas you stand perplexed, especially at the sight of men's sin, uncertain whether to combat it by force or by humble love. Always decide, "I will combat it by humble love." . . . Loving humility is a terrible force; it is strongest of all things and there is nothing like it.[103]

With this crucial element we finally see revealed the intention of the elder: to heal and give hope, even when this demands obedience. It is this humble love in the relationship which protects the freedom of the directee. "The task of the spiritual father is not to destroy a man's freedom, but to assist him to see the truth for himself . . . to discover himself . . . to become what he really is."[104]

If the history of eldership has taught us this, it has also pointed to the possiblity that the director/directee relationship — like any relationship — can also become negative. We must now turn to the problems and dangers which can occur as we traverse the *inner way.*

## 7. On Both Sides: The Absence of Development of the Relationship

The literature dealing with eldership is surprisingly candid about the aberrations in attitude and actions on the part of either director or directee which can make it impossible for an honest relationship to exist. How does one determine if a potential spiritual director is qualified?

102. Brock, *Syriac Fathers,* 88.

103. Fyodor Dostoyevsky, "Discourses and Sermons of Father Zossima," in *The Brothers Karamazov,* trans. Constance Garnett (Middlesex, Eng.: Penguin Books, 1970), 376.

104. Ware, "Spiritual Father," 308.

How does one ensure that the relationship remains proper once it is established?

William McNamara enumerates five qualities which should be sought when establishing a proper relationship with a spiritual director: (1) personal prayer and holiness, (2) reverence for the mystery of every human person, (3) prudence, (4) experience, and (5) learning. He warns the potential directee to reconsider should he or she find any of these wanting.[105] Otherwise he might find himself being governed by "pseudo-eldership," where "the will of one person is enslaved by the will of another, contrary to the counsel of the Apostle Paul: 'Ye are bought with a price, be ye not servants of men' (1 Cor. 7.23)."[106] In such a situation, the directee may well find him- or herself in a protracted period of despondency and oppression which stands in stark contrast to the situation under a true elder:

> A true grace-filled attitude of an Elder, although based upon unconditional obedience, does not deprive a person of the feeling of joy and freedom in God, because he is not in submission to the will of man, but through it to the will of God.[107]

Whereas such an elder is the bearer of God's will, the pseudo-elder overshadows God himself.[108] St. Ignatius Brianchaninov states that in the absence of a good, experienced director, one is better to be without one altogether:

> It is a terrible business to take upon oneself duties of eldership, which can be carried out only by the order of the Holy Spirit and by the action of the Spirit. It is a terrible thing to pretend to be a vessel of the Holy Spirit. . . . Such hypocrisy is terrible. It is disastrous both for oneself and one's neighbor. St. Poemen ordered that a penitent should immediately break with an Elder if living with him proved to be harmful to his soul.[109]

St. Symeon the New Theologian warns that it is harmful to have an elder who tries to teach without having first been a student, and

105. William McNamara, *Christian Mysticism: A Psychotheology* (Chicago: Franciscan Herald Press, 1981), 51.

106. Kontzevitch, "Eldership," 40.

107. *Ibid.*

108. *Ibid.*

109. Kontzevitch, "Eldership," 37, citing St. Ignatius Brianchaninov's *Works,* 1.545.

makes of this an absolute prerequisite, "lest they wander off and lose themselves by speaking of things outside their experience. This is the fate of men who trust in themselves."[110] Even more forcefully he advises potential directees:

> Do not surrender yourself to a master without experience, or to one still subject to the passions, because he might initiate you into the diabolical life instead of the evangelical. Good masters give good doctrine, but evil [ones] teach evil. Bad seeds always produce rotten fruit.[111]

His counsel is to obey such elders only in those matters which do not conflict with the law of God: "On no account obey what is evil . . . and do not be carried away by advice which impresses you greatly at the start."[112] For such first impressions may mean either that the directee lacks the experience not to fall under their sway, or that the advice gratifies some hidden passion within him- or herself.

What is one to do, then, if a proper spiritual director cannot be found? St. Nilus Sorsky accepts the advice of the holy fathers and orders that we "turn to the Scriptures and listen to the Lord himself speaking."[113] Christians have always been guided and "directed" by the Scriptures — as well as by the many classics of spiritual literature which we have quoted abundantly in this work. Yet it is clear that danger also lurks in substituting these for a personal relationship, for "the *starets* [elder] adapts his guidance to the inward state of each," whereas books are limited to offering "the same advice to everyone."[114] In the absence of a qualified director, how can one discern whether a particular text is applicable to his or her predicament? "Even if one cannot find a spiritual father in the full sense, he should at least try to find someone more experienced than himself, able to guide him in his reading," suggests Bishop Kallistos Ware.[115]

In the absence of a personal elder, one can turn to a religious

110. St. Symeon the New Theologian, *The Practical Chapters* (Kalamazoo, MI: Cistercian Publications, 1982), 33-34.

111. *Ibid.*

112. Kontzevitch, "Eldership," 41, citing St. Ignatius Brianchaninov's *Works*, 1.545.

113. St. Nilus Sorsky, "The Monastic Rule," in *A Treasury of Russian Spirituality*, Collected Works of George P. Fedotov, 2 (Belmont, MA: Nordland, 1975), 96.

114. Ware, "Spiritual Father," 309.

115. *Ibid.*

*community*, which embodies, through its ongoing life, the accumulated teachings and guidance of the elders who first laid its foundations. "A well-organized monastery," St. Nilus observes,

> embodies, in an accessible form, the inherited wisdom of many *startsi.* Not only monks, but those who come as visitors for a longer or shorter period, can be formed and guided by the experience of community life.[116]

Many people limit their hope of ever finding a suitable director by expecting him to fit a particular type. Thus they miss those whom God actually sends to them. "There are numerous priests and laymen who, while lacking the more spectacular endowments of the elders, are certainly able to provide others the guidance that they require."[117] How many people have rejected important advice on no other grounds than that they did not want to hear the message which they knew a director would give!

> And so they look for a *deus ex machina* who, by a single miraculous word, will suddenly make everything easy. Such people need to be helped to an understanding of the true nature of spiritual direction.[118]

As we have already stated, even when one has a good spiritual director, one must never think that his advice is a reflection of himself; he too, is an imperfect vehicle of God's Spirit, and liable to mistakes — whereas *sound* advice comes only from God. A good example of this understanding is found in St. Macarius of Optino's *Russian Letters of Spiritual Direction:*

> You say that I helped your aunt. That cannot be. Only the mistakes are mine. All good advice is the advice of the Spirit of God; his advice which I have heard rightly and have passed on without distorting it.[119]

He follows with words which show both the reciprocity involved in the intimate relationship of spiritual direction and the director's human limitations:

116. Cited in Ware, "Spiritual Father," 310.
117. *Ibid.*
118. *Ibid.*, 311.
119. St. Macarius, *Russian Letters,* 26.

> I shall try to answer you as best I can, but you must pray. Pray that God may grant me the ability to say the right words which will bring you help. Pray too, that he will grant you the right faith. . . . No good can come of this letter without his special help.[120]

In order for a spiritual director to serve as an instrument of God's Spirit, certain qualifications were — and are — required. Alan Jones has gleaned five of these from the Eastern Christian tradition. "The first is *love:* not any kind of love, but an openness and readiness to accept another into one's heart. It is a love that takes time and is open to the possible anguish involved."[121] The spiritual director must always be a "lover," holding his or her friends in constant intercession with God's love:

> To say that the first requirement is love is saying a great deal more than our adopting a sentimental attitude. When a Christian loves, he or she is sharing in a divine activity, for love is the work of the Holy Spirit.[122]

Jones's second requirement is *discernment,* which he defines as the capacity "to be both penitential and joyful at the same time: penitential because we discern how far we have fallen short of the glory of God; joyful because the glory outshines our failure to honor it." He adds that "the gift of discernment must always be exercised within the context of love. Without love, discernment can be destructive."[123]

Jones concedes that his third requirement should appear obvious: *patience;* nevertheless, it is difficult to "sit and wait," and quick decisions often prove either too relaxed or too harsh. He quotes St. John Cassian's wisdom, "Severity and harshness never changed anyone."[124]

Fourth, Jones enjoins *frankness and honesty* on both sides of the relationship: "It requires naked trust . . . [to] set the tone of a relationship and . . . [to] allow both to go very deep, beyond mere reaction to the impulses, drives and energies which stir us up."[125]

Finally, there is *detachment,* another rendering of the Greek term

120. *Ibid.*
121. *Exploring Spiritual Direction* (San Francisco: Harper & Row, 1982), 77.
122. *Ibid.*, 78.
123. *Ibid.*
124. *Ibid.*
125. *Ibid.*, 79.

*apatheia* which we discussed as "passionlessness." Jones sees it as the element which prevents the relationship from falling into the "subjectivity of sentimentality":

> The Eastern tradition demands that the spiritual director be willing to embrace solitude and cultivate "detachment" so that he or she may be more available to what God, the Holy Spirit, is doing in the individual heart.[126]

Another modern writer who deals with the history of spiritual direction is Jordan Aumann. Although he does not write about the Eastern tradition specifically, his treatment of the intimate relationship required in spiritual direction has much to commend it. He opens with a definition: "Spiritual direction is the art of leading souls progressively from the beginning of the spiritual life to the height of Christian perfection." It is, he says, a very particular ministry — a "practical science" — whose goal is "appropriation" — "appl[ying] to a particular case the principles of theology." Furthermore, it is of necessity progressive: "Direction should begin as soon as the soul has definitely resolved to travel along the road to Christian perfection, and should continue through all phases of that journey."[127] The protracted nature of the ministry places certain demands on the director, which Aumann categorizes as follows: "Technical Qualities" which include learning, prudence, and experience; "Moral Qualities" which include piety, zeal for the sanctification of souls, humility, and disinterestedness (which sounds somewhat like *apatheia*) — all serving to protect the relationship.[128]

He also imposes certain duties on both parties. The director must (1) manifest a profound *knowledge* of the soul he is directing — its character, temperament (positive and negative), inclinations, likes, dislikes, etc.; (2) offer cogent *instruction* to help the directee solve his or her own problems whenever possible; (3) provide *encouragement* to infuse in the directee an optimistic confidence in God and a healthy distrust of him- or herself; (4) exercise *control* over the spiritual life of the directee to the degree that important steps are never taken without first being submitted

126. *Ibid.*

127. Jordan Aumann, *Spiritual Theology* (Westminster, MD: Christian Classics, 1987), 380.

128. *Ibid.*, 382-87.

to the dialogue; (5) *correct* his or her defects while maintaining "sweetness of character"; (6) maintain *progression* in the course of the direction, "accommodating" it to the "temperament, age, and circumstances of life" of the directee; and (7) observe *confidentiality,* not only to preserve the directee's trust, but also because "many of these things are in some way connected with the internal forum," and their becoming publicly known would result in nothing more than "morbid curiosity."[129]

The directee's duties include (1) *sincerity,* since without it, *ab initio,* no direction is possible; although the spiritual director need not also be a person's confessor, he will find it impossible to offer direction if he knows nothing of the directee's sins and imperfections; (2) *obedience,* meaning that while the two are indeed traveling together, they "are *not* on equal footing"; (3) *perseverance,* without which direction is "rendered sterile," since he or she may too frequently change directors; and (4) *discretion,* meaning that the directee should never reveal to others the particular counsel received, since "it is given to a particular person in light of *particular* circumstances, and does not apply to other persons living in other circumstances."[130]

In the Russian novelist Dostoyevsky's fictional image of the elder are embodied all the qualities we have been discussing. The starets Zossima in *The Brothers Karamazov* is modelled after the elder Amvrossy whom the author visited at the Optino Monastery. His portrait also incorporates qualities associated with such elders of the Russian tradition as Seraphim of Sarov; Leonid, Makary, and Nektary of Optino; and John of Kronstadt — characteristics which, he says, "evolved in the East from a practice that today goes back over a thousand years":

> What, then, is such an Elder? An Elder was one who took your soul and your will into his soul and will. When you choose an Elder, you renounce your own will and yield it to him in complete submission, complete self-abnegation. This "novitiate," this terrible school of abnegation, is undertaken voluntarily . . . in the hope of self-conquest, of self-mastery, in order that, after a life of obedience, he will attain to perfect freedom, that is to say, freedom from self. In this way, he escapes the fate of those who have lived their whole life without *finding their selves within themselves.*[131]

129. *Ibid.,* 391-93.
130. *Ibid.*
131. "Elders," in *Brothers Karamazov,* 28.

## 8. The Penitential Tradition of the Inner Way

Before turning from history to contemporary practice, we must examine briefly the penitential tradition and discipline of the Church. As throughout our exploration, our study will be limited to the confines of ministry, avoiding long tangents into history, canon law, and liturgical ritual per se. Again, such discussions are best left to the appropriate scholars. One such person is Prof. John H. Erickson, who in a recent article in the *St. Vladimir's Theological Quarterly* produced a very succinct overview from which I will draw heavily, while selectively, and to which I refer the reader who wishes to learn more.[132]

The fate of penitential practices across long centuries of Eastern Christian history and canon law, as Erickson indicates, is complex; "no other sacramental act of the church has undergone such extensive developments and changes in its outward forms." Down through the fourth century there was a clear eucharistic emphasis; ἐξομολογῆσις [*exomologēsis:* "confession"] had not yet become a juridical procedure, but was treated (as I have suggested it should still be) as the "fruit" of the work of repentance, and affording the means for sinners to return to the Eucharist. "There was likewise no set formula for 'Absolution,' . . . often one simply reads that a person is to proceed to communion." The reconciliation of apostates occupied such a large concern in this period that their treatment became the *model* for the sacrament of confession/absolution.

But in the Byzantine period,

> we are in quite a different world, the world of monasticism and asceticism, the world of "spiritual counsel and direction" under the guidance of the πνευματικὸς πάτερ (the spiritual father), the world whose chief theoreticians . . . viewed the essence of the Christian life as a gradual purification through a "spiritual therapy."

It came to be accepted in this period that the faithful undertake spiritual "work" under the direction of an elder; disputes broke out as monastic and nonmonastic traditions clashed over who should direct this "spiritual therapy." By the time of Iconoclasm, the monks obtained "a monopoly in penitential matters," serving as "confessors" for the laity, but

132. John H. Erickson, "Penitential Discipline in the Orthodox Canonical Tradition," *St. Vladimir's Theological Quarterly* 21.4 (1977), 191-206.

only after securing "appropriate letters of commission from the hierarchial authority." Penances were viewed as medicinal rather than vindictive or punitive, and the growing corpus of penitential rules was typically interpreted with sensitivity rather than literally and legalistically; the rules themselves always seemed to provide, Erickson observes, an "escape clause," indicating that their intent was to heal and reconcile. He cites the 102nd canon of the Council in Trullo:

> It is incumbent upon those who have received from God the power to bind and loose . . . to apply medicine suitable to the disease, lest . . . he should fail to heal the sick man. For the disease of sin is not simple, but various and multiform, and it germinates many mischievous offshoots . . . until it is checked by the power of the physician.

As the *praxis* of healing gained importance, the example of the monastery influenced confession, and the novices' examination yielded a ready model for "gentle exploration of spiritual ills on the part of the Confessor . . . [through] lists of questions."

It was in the post-Byzantine period that penitential practices began to be attended by many of their current problems. Thus in seventeenth-century Russia, sacramental confession came to be viewed as a formal "obligation" qualifying the person for his second yearly obligation — reception of the Eucharist — which together rendered him a "member in good standing of the church community." Indeed, these obligations came to be civil requirements as well as ecclesiastical ones, and fines were levied on those failing to comply. Juridicism was introduced, best seen in the substitution of the Latin formula "I absolve thee . . ." for the traditional Greek formula "May God forgive thee . . ." in absolution. Writes Erickson, "confession and absolution remain, but too often they are quite removed from the idea of repentance and forgiveness of sin."

Erickson ends by questioning whether a "gap" exists in present-day discipline of *metanoia* between the formal rite of confession/absolution and the reality which that discipline ought to reflect. Is healing and reconciliation truly happening? History would seem to suggest otherwise. A renaissance of spiritual direction is clearly called for. The gap must be closed. The *inner way* must again be entered.

# 3 The Spiritual Component: Exploring the Theological Roots of Spiritual Direction

*Now is the time, O my soul, to know yourself and your destiny. Look to yourself, O my soul. Yield not to fatigue.*

St. Gregory Nazianzen

*He who knows himself knows everything.*

St. Anthony the Great

## Introduction: Distinguishing the "Spiritual" and the "Direction"

While examining the historical tradition in the previous chapter, our orientation was toward the present and the future. We examined only those parts of the rich heritage of eldership which could speak to our contemporary situation. Thus it was not a history as such but a kind of preamble to what remains to be studied, for there is no way to approach spiritual direction as a viable contemporary ministry without gaining some grounding in what has gone before.

The first task we confront as we turn to contemporary spiritual direction is to distinguish between the two elements in the phrase. That is, I propose to examine the various *theological* issues surrounding this ministry in conjunction with the adjective "spiritual," and the *therapeu-*

*tic* and *psychological* issues in connection with the noun "direction." Although the two cannot be distinguished in the *praxis* of ministry, this approach affords a handy matrix for examining the various dimensions of this ministry.

It also provides an order of priority for that examination. In English, the adjective precedes the noun it modifies, and this fits nicely with my own view of spiritual direction as a whole. Everything we seek to do in order to heal and reconcile people — the methodology — proceeds out of our view of what God and humankind are — our theological "roots" and Christian anthropology. In the end, I think, we will see what a difference this makes in the *praxis* itself, as we are able to distinguish spiritual direction from other forms of guidance, counsel, and psychotherapy.

What, then, do we mean by "theological roots"? The term "theology" in Greek is a composite of two terms: θεός [*Theos:* "God"] and λόγος [*logos:* "word"]; it is, thus, literally a "word about God." We will thus examine those areas in spiritual direction which particularly lend themselves to hearing such a "word about God" and examine a variety of theological concerns which comprise the "spiritual" component of spiritual direction.

## 1. Fragmentation and Transformation: Life out of the Compost Heap

Our first theological concern is identified with the ancient motif of *fragmentation* and *transformation.* Crises abound in human life, and although spiritual direction is never limited to dealing with them, it may well be *initiated* by an individual's experience of such a crisis; or again a new crisis might arise while one is already engaged in spiritual direction, and thus would naturally be introduced to the dialogue. Whatever the circumstances, however, crises do appear in a person's life as a veritable "death," a disintegration of life. At such times God speaks to interpret our fragmentation — and begin our transformation.

Vilma Seelaus sets the stage for our understanding:

> Fragmentation, the crisis of identity and meaning, touches the lives of each of us. Yet the potential for growth and transformation inher-

> ent in life's struggles and breakdowns evades most of us. We fail to realize that *dark times condition us for God* — that they invite us to a transformed identity through a deeper faith, hope, and love.[1]

We have seen in history how vitally important are faith, hope, and love in providing a path to healing and reconciliation, and that it takes a spiritual director to help us understand our situation and struggle to overcome it. In crisis situations it is particularly necessary that one be guided to understand the basic theological teaching of "synergy" (divine and human "cooperation") that we alone cannot cure ourselves, but also that God will not "break down the door" to force his way into our lives; he knocks at the door, to be sure, but then waits for us to open it. Divine grace and human will must work together for transformation to occur. It is the director's task to see that this theological lesson is learned by the directee who may be experiencing such a crisis.

Seelaus makes this point in a striking manner by turning to nature, and finding there a most apt — if unexpected — example: "Something as simple as the *compost heap,* familiar to organic gardeners, powerfully symbolizes the reality of God at work in human life crises." For non-organic gardeners and others, this is what is meant:

> To build a compost heap one gathers organic material like weeds, leaves, vegetable and fruit peelings — and manure if possible. These are heaped up with layers of soil. . . . Gradually, the contents begin to break down.

With diligent work, digging, probing, and turning over the ingredients, "rich, dark earth" is the eventual result, and

> the compost heap has risen to new life! In dying to its own life, the banana peels, and all the stuff of the compost heap, can now enrich new life.[2]

This same process occurs throughout nature: a buried seed bursts apart in order to bring forth a tree; a caterpillar buries itself in a hard case in order to be transformed into a butterfly; a baby is forced out of its mother's womb in order to assume an identity of its own. Each of

1. Vilma Seelaus, "Fragmentation and Divine Transformation," *The Way* (Oct. 1988), 301.

2. *Ibid.*

these natural phenomena includes a form of death — a separation, a fragmentation, a loss. Something old must give way, must die, in order for new life to emerge. Disintegration and fragmentation precede rebirth.

When disintegration and fragmentation disrupt our lives, when the "dark times" are upon us, when we or our loved ones experience illness or broken relationships, failure, or even death, our first inclination is to flee the situation. At this point we need a spiritual director to work diligently with us, probing and turning over the depths of our being, in order to produce "rich, dark earth." History tells us that he will probably counsel us to remain still and resist the impulse to flee. He will summon all that he has learned through his *own* sufferings in order to bear witness to the eternal truth: that an even deeper communion with God can emerge from the fragmentation of what used to be. As T. S. Eliot muses in his *Four Quartets:*

> We must be still, and still moving
> Into another intensity
> For a further union, a deeper communion.[3]

When we near the brink of panic and fear, the spiritual director will remind us that it is possible to *endure* — "to be still, and yet still moving." Because of his theological training he will affirm that all that is comfortable, everything familiar, those things in this world to which we cling, must always give way. Great religious anthropologists like Mircea Eliade have demonstrated that the universal life-death-resurrection cycle represents the deepest reality of life.[4] Whether by the biblical parable of the seed falling on the earth or Seelaus's graphic image of the compost heap, we learn that if we are to grow into deeper communion with God, we must accept — and in a sense even "befriend" — the diminishments of life inherent in such circumstances.

The director undoubtedly will also remind us that the Cross itself was a quintessentially "dark time," embodying *every* dark time that will ever be faced by a Christian. Indeed, the paschal mystery of Jesus Christ is a unique manifestation of the cosmic process which has been part of

3. T. S. Eliot, "East Coker," in *Four Quartets* (New York: Harcourt, Brace & World, 1943), 32.

4. See Mircea Eliade, *The Sacred and the Profane* (New York: Harcourt, Brace & World, 1959). Also his many other books which point to this same motif.

the universe *ab origine;* its uniqueness lies in the fact that the Author himself entered nature and sanctified it by filling it with himself.

> The death and resurrection of Jesus Christ holds before us the truth of God's abiding presence and transforming activity in all of life. This is particularly true in human relations.[5]

Looking to the Cross, we understand what Seelaus meant about being "conditioned for God," finding "potential for growth and transformation," and obtaining a "transformed identity through a deeper faith, hope, and love."

It is imperative for the spiritual director to be adequately trained in theology, for unless he himself *understands* these lessons, he will not be able to *transmit* them effectively to a directee at that moment of crisis when he or she is most open to receiving it. Theology teaches us that inner spiritual transformation is brought about when one's heart remains open to God's grace, which seeks ever to enter it (Rom. 5.5). Examples abound for the director to use in urging directees to keep an open heart in the face of fragmentation. The ancient patriarch Job is a wonderful — and most *human* one. No matter how badly we may be broken, we can identify with him. And what is the theological lesson of this "righteous servant of God," abandoned, dejected, isolated, and accused, but who eventually beheld God's glory? Never did Job curse or deny God. He was in pain and crisis — fragmented — and he *knew* it. So did his wife and friends. But Job refused to close his heart during the "dark times." With resignation he could say, "The Lord gives and the Lord takes away," and then in triumph follow this with, "Blessed be the name of the Lord" — *in any case!*

For the Christian, the ultimate image of facing up to dark times is found in the Cross and Resurrection of Christ. The director must teach that our individual crosses can no more be by-passed or denied than could the Lord's. As he faced his Cross squarely, so we too must "take up" our life crises if we hope to be returned to life again. We must "pass through" our crises rather than flee or deny them. We cannot "dig out" unless we first "dig in." The great desert father, St. Anthony of Egypt, knowing that healing and reconciliation — true Christian growth — occur only in this way, stated that, "He who knows himself,

5. Seelaus, "Fragmentation," 302.

knows everything." St. Peter of Damascus concurred: "To him who has come to know himself is given the knowledge of all things." And St. Gregory of Nazianzus counselled an enthusiastic, untiring search within oneself: "Now is the time, O my soul, to know yourself and your destiny. . . . Look to yourself, O my soul. Yield not to fatigue."[6]

Such penetration of one's inner depths is best undertaken with the trust, counsel, and guidance of a spiritual director. Although a dangerous undertaking, to be sure, it is the only way for healing and restoration to occur, for new life to emerge from fragmentation. He will help us not only to find the sins which lurk within us, but also to discover the great reservoir of God's healing grace which abides within us.[7] This realization will bring to life for us the meaning of the verses which are so often beautifully sung in the liturgy of the Eastern Church: "Out of the depths have I cried, O Lord!" (Ps. 130.1) and "Deep calls unto deep" (Ps. 42.8). In our own fragmentation we understand these cries of anguish, uttered long ago by the Psalmist as he begged for that healing and reconciliation which can come only from the God who dwells in the depths of each human being. We hear these words anew and listen, and obey. We enter into our own depths in a state of fragmentation, but in seeking transformation, we shift our "center" from our depths to the depths of the compassionate God whom we encounter within. After all, theology teaches us that healing is God's activity, and it is God's will if we allow him to use our brokenness to bring forth new life. Our spiritual director can remind us of this in many ways: in Seelaus's image of the decomposing compost heap — so effective because it is so unexpected; in the soil, broken to bring forth new fruit; in the eucharistic bread, broken to bring forth the food of eternity; in the Σταυρόμενος [*Stauromenos:* "the One on the Cross"], broken to bring forth eternal life and resurrection. Our spiritual director can help us see that God will use the brokenness of our own "dark times" to produce the transformation we seek — but only if we are willing to let him.

6. See Metr. Philip Saliba and Joseph J. Allen (eds.), *Out of the Depths Have I Cried* (Brookline, MA: Holy Cross Press, 1979), 3. These quotations indicate the presence and activity of God within one's depths. The orientation of the book is phenomenological and meditative, the appropriate orientation to describe this truth. In the closing section of this chapter, we shall turn to "the place of the heart," which carries the same meaning as one's depths.

7. *Ibid.,* 18-19.

## 2. Covenantal Suppositions: The God-Issue

The second theological concern in spiritual direction hinges on the *covenant,* that relationship which God has initiated with his people. For Christians this implies the message of both the Old and New Testaments. I call this the "God-issue" in spiritual direction. The scriptural scholar Walter Brueggemann offers us a starting point in a discussion of scripture and ministry:

> The primary claim of "covenant" as a way of understanding the theme of pastoral counsel . . . is that "human persons are grounded in Another who initiates personhood and who stays bound to persons in loyal ways for their well-being." This is, of course, a way of saying that human beings have to do fundamentally with God.

According to the Eastern Christian tradition, one must immediately interject the qualification that the God with whom human persons "have to do fundamentally" is a *very specific* and *identifiable* God, One who revealed himself fully in Jesus Christ and the Holy Spirit. Brueggemann continues:

> Covenant is the deep and pervasive affirmation that our lives in all aspects depend upon our relatedness to this other One who retains initiative in our lives (sovereignty), and who wills more good for us than we do for ourselves (graciousness; cf. Eph. 3.20).[8]

If covenant indeed means that a person is grounded and finds his or her true identity in that "Other" who is God, then the proper question of "identity" for us to ask is not only "Who am I?" but "To Whom do I belong?" It is no easy task today for the spiritual director to transmit this truth to his directee; there is a temptation in modern society to follow the way, not of "God-groundedness," but of "self-groundedness." Donald Gowan has investigated this conflict at length, and concludes that the modern human being believes that life springs from itself, and that the human generates his own power and vitality.[9]

The truth is that human beings regularly fall into a dilemma of

8. Walter Brueggemann, "Covenanting as Human Vocation," *Interpretation: A Journal of Bible and Theology* 33.2 (1979), 116.

9. See Donald Gowan, *When Man Becomes God* (Pittsburgh: Pickwick Press, 1975).

extremes. Either they believe that as individuals they are totally self-sufficient (and these are destined sooner or later to discover that this is *never* true) or that they have no sufficiency to act at all — something so irresponsible that no one must ever be allowed to believe it! Only by accepting the truth of covenant will we recognize that, because human life is grounded in a relationship with God, we are bound to take certain initiatives in life. Our historical reflections reminded us that we must never *assume* that God will do anything for us unless we perform our own part.

While Eastern Christian theology has traditionally labeled the human response-to-God as "synergy," it could just as well be termed a covenantal relationship. The reality is the same. However it is spoken of, this reality lies at the very starting point of spiritual direction. Brueggemann explains why:

> The abandonment of God in modern psychology has likely been because of authoritarian or irrelevant caricatures of God. But if we are to build a fresh conversation between Bible and pastoral care, we must abandon such caricatures and learn to speak about the faithful covenanting One for whom the Bible makes claim.[10]

Likewise, we can state that a "fresh conversation" is needed between the covenantal relationship and the contemporary practice of spiritual direction. What, for instance, are the claims of the "God-issue" to which human beings must respond? What are the claims which must be kept solidly within the director/directee dialogue? Four are obvious.

First, the covenant-making God possesses the power to *make things new.*[11] This belongs to him uniquely. He has entrusted it to no other being, but he gives it as a gift to all living things. Paul Tournier states that all newness in our lives is a gift from the Other One (see Mt. 7.11, Eph. 2.8, and Jas. 1.17), and demonstrates that only God's gift-giving can break down the vicious cycles of "grudge and isolation" which vitiate our existence; these always impede the ability to truly give gifts to one another.[12]

The second claim is that the covenant-making God brings this

10. Brueggemann, "Covenanting," 117.

11. See Walter Brueggemann, *The Prophetic Imagination* (Philadelphia: Fortress, 1978).

12. See Paul Tournier, *The Meaning of Gifts* (Richmond, VA: John Knox, 1964).

newness of life into being *by speech.*[13] Eastern Christian theology emphasis states that God's creation *ex nihilo* was accomplished by his Λόγος [*Logos:* "Word"]. Brueggemann echoes this truth: "Covenant does not happen in silence. The metaphor of covenant presumes that this other One speaks, and by his speech things are changed."[14] When God does speak, it is a "self-announcement," one which promises his *fidelity* to those whom he has created in his own image. In the scriptures this is no small matter. None of the other "gods" has a decisive word to speak, and so they remain silent (see Is. 41.26-29). Only the One True God cares infinitely and radically for human life — and he says so through his Word. The multitude of modern "gods" likewise are mute.

The third claim is that God *holds his covenant partner to himself,* such that the life of the other is ordained to deal with God. The spiritual director must never forget this particular claim, for it not only declares that "I will be your God," but also demands that "You will be my people"; "I have called you by name. You are mine" (Is. 43.1). The theological importance of this assertion has to do with creation itself. God claims us simultaneously with giving us life, not at some point after we have already come to exist. Before he claims us *we are not.* We possess no identity outside God's claim on us. We *are* what we were created to *be* only when we are related to the God who seeks to hold us in this "bond."

The fourth and final claim is that the covenantal bonding of the God/man relationship *re-defines* human life. It sets the person in a new context of "surprise and amazement," for it is summed up in the radical message which Jesus Christ sent to John the Baptist in prison: "the blind receive their sight, the lame walk, the lepers are cleansed, the deaf hear, the dead are raised . . ." (Lk. 7.22).[15] Within the covenant God is no silent, passive upholder of things; he is an active agent — acting on our behalf. The spiritual director cannot afford to forget to impress this on his directee, for in Brueggemann's words, his very task "involves bringing persons to such a knowledge of self in the presence of God."[16]

The claims of the "God-issue" carry implications for the *practice* of spiritual direction. Brueggemann holds that "sound human psychology must ask about responding and responsive actions appropriate to

13. See Peter Hodgson, *Jesus, Word and Presence* (Philadelphia: Fortress, 1981).
14. Brueggemann, "Covenanting," 119.
15. *Ibid.,* 121.
16. *Ibid.*

God's initiative toward us,[17] so it is appropriate to ask, "How is the directee to be counseled and guided in order to participate in this relationship with God?" and "How should he or she respond?"

First, in response to the One who *"makes all things new,"* the faithful human response is to *hope.* We are summoned to function in hope every day, trusting that God's promises and purposes for our life will ultimately not fail. The spiritual director must give special attention to this, since our limited faculties do not allow us fully to *see* God's way.[18] According to the elders, *despair* and chronic dejection — the sin of ἀθυμία [*athymia:* "faintheartedness"] always militates against hope. Brueggemann's perceptive observation is apt:

> I submit that despair and its psychologically acceptable form, depression, are in fact covert acts of atheism in which we conclude nothing can happen apart *from* us, and no one is at work *in* us![19]

In theological terms, despair is a modern form of the ancient heresy known as Pelagianism, for it depends on self-will alone.

In response to the *"One who speaks,"* the faithful human response is to *listen.* Good listening is not easy. It requires that we concede that we are subject to Another who addresses us by name and identifies us as one of his creatures. It means yielding to him before we act. Brueggemann reminds us that in the Bible "there is, of course, no more sustained prophetic indictment than, 'You did not listen'" (Jer. 5.21, 7.13, 11.10).[20] In spiritual direction we see the dangerous attitude, "There is no one but me," manifested in the directee's failure to listen: he or she always speaks, always seizes the initiative, always insists on self-definition. Good listening is not easy, but must be learned, a subject we shall investigate in more depth in a later chapter.

To the God who *"holds us to himself,"* the faithful human response entails *obedient action.* The directee must struggle to *do* justice and righteousness, to *live* in loyalty and integrity. It means, as Brueggemann says, answering with "the fullness of maturity to which we are invited"[21] or, in St. Paul words, "unto the measure of the stature of the fullness of

17. *Ibid.*
18. See Jürgen Moltmann, *Theology of Hope* (New York: Harper & Row, 1967).
19. Brueggemann, "Covenanting," 121.
20. *Ibid.*
21. *Ibid.*, 122.

Christ" (Eph. 4.13). Only if we are spiritually mature can we live our lives in gratitude and love for, and obedience to, the God who constantly reveals to us *who we are.*

For the spiritual director it should be clear that each of these faithful human responses is in fact, as Brueggemann states, "a protest against self-groundedness," for "the self-grounded person is finally (a) hopeless, (b) must always do the speaking, and (c) hears nothing to which to make answer."[22] History has shown us that in order to be healed, in order to be transformed from his or her state of fragmentation, the directee must exercise "synergy," or in terms of the "God-issue" just discussed, must be led into active participation in that faithful covenantal relationship which God himself established. He or she must *experience* it in a daily struggle.

## 3. Theology and Experience

Our third theological concern deals with the relationship of *experience* to theology along the *inner way.* How is the spiritual director to bring the light of theology to bear on experiences of fragmentation such as we have been discussing? Several contemporary authors have addressed this question. Their input can augment that of the elders, and lead us deeper into the "spiritual" component of spiritual direction.

Dermot Lane opens with a word of caution:

> God comes to man *in* experience. We receive God in experience. We do not project, create, or posit God in experience. Rather, we find God already there *ahead* of us, in human experience,

then goes on to define what we have called the "word about God" in these same terms:

> Theology, from beginning to end, is about the critical unpacking of the revelation of God that takes place in human experience through faith.[23]

Compare this with the position of William A. Barry and William J. Connolly:

22. *Ibid.*
23. *The Experience of God* (New York: Paulist Press, 1981), 3.

> Religious experience is to spiritual direction what foodstuff is to cooking. Without foodstuff there can be no cooking. Without religious experience there can be no spiritual direction.[24]

This is not to say that human experience stands alone. It requires the spiritual director's *theological interpretation,* or what David Tracy aptly terms the "Christian fact," which must be one of the principal sources of theology alongside "contemporary experience."[25] When a director helps his directee interpret his or her own experience against the "Christian fact," God finds a means of speaking, and the experience, whatever its nature, becomes a "religious" experience. Bernard Lonergan adds that the phenomenon of *repeated experiences,* observed by director and directee alike in the extended process of dialogue, can be a sign that God desires an avenue of entrance into the person's life:

> Experience, especially *repeated* experience, of one's frailty or wickedness, raises the question of one's salvation and, on a more fundamental level, there arises the question of God.[26]

Finally, Edward Schillebeeckx touches the crux of the matter of applying theology to experience when he states: "The world of human experience is the only access to the saving reality of revelation and faith."[27] We can listen to a revelation from God only if it falls within our own realm of experience.

All of these factors raise some obvious problems for spiritual direction. If indeed no experience stands alone but each requires theological interpretation in order to lead to healing and reconciliation, what happens if the spiritual director lacks the acumen to "read" the experiences properly, or the facility to explain them to the directee in terms he or she can understand?

First, the directee might fall into the danger of "subjective emotionalism." Knowing only that he wants *something* to be, something to happen, he may be left with just a fleeting experience, a passing mood. He might even impose his own "God-words" and "religious talk" on the

24. *The Practice of Spiritual Direction* (San Francisco: Harper & Row, 1982), 8.

25. David Tracy, *Blessed Rage of Order* (New York: Seabury, 1975), 43.

26. Bernard Lonergan, *Method in Theology* (London: Darton, Longman and Todd, 1972), 39.

27. Edward Schillebeeckx, "Faith Functioning in Human Self-Understanding," in *The Word in History,* ed. T. Burke (New York: Sheed & Ward, 1966), 45.

experience in an effort to make some sense of it. The theologically astute director will see this as manipulation and offer corrections.

As dangerous is the opposite tendency, extreme "objectivity." If the directee cannot find meaning in an experience unless it be empirically verified, clinically and objectively, he or she may well exclude the inherent mystery through which God can gain entrance. Human interpretation is by definition limited by what our senses can perceive and our minds can grasp, but room must always be left for that which lies beyond our limitations. The theologically astute director is obligated to introduce this element of mystery.

The truth is that the human experience which the directee brings to spiritual direction cannot be reduced to *either* the subjective or the objective. In either extreme God's presence will be held suspect. Either his actions will be excluded, or they will be falsely interpreted. Experience as the proper "foodstuff" of spiritual direction involves both the human subject and the objective reality. The simultaneous presence of both renders each experience in life a true "encounter" with God, and thus a viable place for healing and reconciliation. Lane writes,

> The word "encounter" suggests a degree of contact between the subject and the world. It implies that within the experience we find something already there; we come up against reality as *given* and *prior* to us.[28]

Knowing that his directee (the subject) will inevitably experience movements of awareness, decision, response, reflection, participation, etc. in relationship to the persons and things in his world (the object) — and that it is false and dangerous to polarize the objective and the subjective, the director must integrate the two by evaluating what he hears from his directee against what he knows to be true about God and the world:

> Experience should not be located as something simply within the subject who looks at life, but rather as the product resulting from the *critical interaction* between the subject and reality.[29]

Knowing furthermore that "a basic characteristic of experience is that no one experience discloses the totality of reality,"[30] the director

28. Lane, *Experience,* 8.
29. *Ibid.,* 9.
30. *Ibid.*

will help the directee understand that the patterns and repetitions of experiences which they together observe emerging in the process of dialogue could well be God's means of revealing himself. The experiences of the past — whether in the stories of others or in one's own — have a bearing on how one interprets the experiences of the present. And these, in turn, will bear on how a person will interpret the experiences of the future. Every new discovery, every new insight, gives God a new opportunity to reveal himself.

> Experience, reflected upon in the light of the prophetic word of Scripture in the Church, is a *locus theologicus*, a place where God discloses his ways to man. . . . But we can always trivialize experience by constricting it to our limitations, rather than trying to transcend the limitations of our experience, in order to become aware of the highly diversified ways in which people meet God.[31]

If this be true, then it certainly follows that

> The focus of . . . spiritual direction is on experience, not ideas, and specifically on religious experience, *i.e.,* any experience of the mysterious Other whom we call God. Moreover, this experience is viewed, not as an isolated event, but as an expression of the ongoing personal relationship God has established with each one of us.[32]

Thus we see that affording a proper theological interpretation to human experience is basic and crucial to the "spiritual" component of spiritual direction. Should one by-pass experience — whether positive or negative — one limits the healing possibilities found within the *inner way.*

## 4. Human Choice and Free Will

Our fourth theological concern for contemporary spiritual direction is *human choice* and *free will.* We must recall at the outset the fundamental truth that divine grace has truly penetrated human nature, and remind the spiritual director constantly to transmit this fact to his directee.

31. Michael Ivens, "Healing the Divided Self," *The Way* (1976), 171.
32. Barry and Connolly, *Practice,* 8.

"What are human beings that you are mindful of them, mortals that you care for them?" (Ps. 8.4, quoted in Heb. 2.6). Eastern Christian theology teaches that although God is "mindful" and "caring" about his creation, part of the order of that creation is the free will which he "risked" endowing upon humankind — a free will which can be, and is, used incorrectly, sinfully. At the dawn of time, when proud Adam chose to "become god," he fell from the state of oneness and communion with him, and in the course of his fall became less than human — less than what he was created to be. Today separation from God is not just a memory of that primeval event, but a continuing bondage to evil as a consequence of it. We find ourselves being led in various ways toward sinful acts, isolation, and separation. Furthermore, the conditions which lead us away from God can be either self-caused or imposed from outside. The spiritual director must be conscious of these facts as he sets out to deal with his directee's use, and misuse, of choice and free will.

The paradox of the directee's condition is that so often the very thing that captivates him is at one and the same time that from which he yearns to be free! In short we long for release and deliverance from the very conditions to which we "pledge our allegiance." Our dilemma is further confounded by the fact that while we truly yearn to be free, we fear being discovered, and thus *hide* from the only One who can bring about our restoration, healing, and freedom — the covenant-making God.

The Genesis narrative provides an instructive paradigm. As Adam and Eve rose to consciousness of their prideful choice, their initial response was to "hide among the trees in the Garden." When our spiritual director directs to us the question which God put to our ancestors, "Where are you?" (Gen. 3.9), we too hate to hear it and often hide, even though we know that it is the only question which can lead to restoration.[33] The scriptures further reveal that God was, in fact, "searching" for Adam and Eve in order to restore them. Indeed, his question marked the beginning of salvation history, and Adam's response, "I was afraid

33. God posed this question not because he did not "know" where Adam was, but in order to "bring Adam up," to raise his consciousness (conscience) regarding his action — and that is precisely the point in spiritual direction. God knows all things already, but we must be brought to understanding, like the Prodigal Son who first had to "come to himself" before he could decide to return "home" and be restored.

. . . and I hid myself" (Gen. 3.10) typifies the human experience ever since. It is repeated in Cain's cowardice after committing the first recorded human murder, "Anyone who finds me may kill me" (Gen. 4.14). This type of hiding continues to this day. But God did not relent, and continued to ask, "Where are you?" — to the point of taking on human flesh in the person of Jesus Christ, who identified himself as the one who "came to seek out and to save the lost" (Lk. 19.10).

The truth is that planted deep within the heart of every human person — fearful, in hiding, and resistant as we may be — is a yearning to be healed, to be found, to be restored. Most often the spiritual director will find his directee in precisely this state, not knowing where to turn. The history of eldership has shown us that it is always possible for us to respond to God's grace. We can always break out of evil bondage and resolve our self-imposed predicament. The opportunity exists ἐν δυνάμει [*en dynamei:* "potentially"], and we may choose to "actualize" it by stepping forward and saying "Here I am," even as we acknowledge ourselves to be "undone" — people of unclean lips, dwelling among people of unclean lips (Is. 6.5, 8). On the other hand, we may choose to let it be, to say "No" again, and continue to hide in shame and fear. If we choose the latter route, we will remain in bondage and the newness of life which comes through forgiveness will continue to evade us.

This will place a difficult burden on our spiritual director. Nevertheless, he will persist in a careful and sensitive dialogue to "seek out and save the lost." He will not use force, but in the words of St. Paul, "speak the truth in love" (see Eph. 4.15). If and when he probes our lives in the course of dialogue, he will take into careful account both how he poses his questions and what their focus will be. St. John Chrysostom emphasized the importance of sensitivity in this area in his praise of the careful manner of the Apostle Paul:

> Having first spoken in love which he [Paul] displayed, the love which he bears toward those who are censured, he makes his speech less offensive.[34]

In imitating this approach, we should never err, however, by thinking that what a person has done is of no consequence. The spiritual director's awareness of the reality of sin and misery, of broken relation-

34. St. John Chrysostom, *Homilies on Second Corinthians,* in NPNF, 12.34.

ships and isolation, will prevent him from issuing an "adjustment statement" like "It really doesn't matter, everything will turn out OK." He knows full well — and is obliged to make his directee also know — that what we do *does* matter; it does have consequences. The issue here is that the "what" of the question is indeed an ultimately serious matter, but the "how" of its asking cannot be insensitive or mechanical. The director must make it clear that while he certainly stands against the directee's sin, he nevertheless stands *with* him as a person. The person must be loved even while his sin is hated; the person must feel accepted even while realizing that his sinful behavior is rejected. Unless this understanding pervades the dialogue, it is highly doubtful that the searching question "Where are you?" will ever meet with the desired answer "Here I am"; it is this response which will demonstrate that the directee truly wants to be "found," and that the process of restoration can get under way.

This brings us to the central matter of *choice.* We are constantly making choices, and this practice is always risky. On the one hand lies the danger of "fatalism" and "predeterminism," and on the other, Pelagianism, human willfulness. The spiritual director must remind his directee of how choice is to be utilized from a Christian point of view. In doing so he can best refer to the encyclopedic St. John of Damascus.

St. John refers to the human being as an αὐτεξούσιον [*autexousion:* "one who possesses the will of a reasoning soul"].[35] The human is, in a sense, radically free. He is κύριος πράξεως [*kyrios praxeōs:* "master of actions"]. He can rationally deliberate about those matters which "belong to our nature": growth, generation, etc.[36] Through his creation in the image of God, the human person has been given freedom through λόγος [*logos:* "reason"] and βουλή [*boulē:* "will-power"] in order to make ἐπιλογαί [*epilogai:* "selections"]. These God-given characteristics ensure that the freedom with which a human being chooses is his *own.* He makes choices γνώμη [*gnōmēi:* "by resolution"] on his own volition, never through another's — even that of his spiritual director. If this were not the case, right decisions would hold no "virtue," for as the Damascene emphasizes, "Nothing which is done by force is an act of virtue."[37] It is also

35. See St. John of Damascus, *Vita Barlaam et Joasaph* in PG 96.996-97.

36. See St. John of Damascus, *The Orthodox Faith* 2.25 in his *Writings* in Fathers of the Church, 37 (Washington, DC: Catholic University of America Press, 1958), 255-57.

37. *Ibid.,* 236.

important to realize that the freedom by which choices are made is neither an abstraction nor a philosophical proposition, but something which the person truly *has:*

> Free will is absolutely inherent in every rational creature. . . . After all, of what good can rationality be to a nature that does not reason freely?[38]

That a person can choose incorrectly and fall into sin is also discussed at length by St. John, and must be understood in the practice of spiritual direction. The starting point in the Eastern Christian teaching is that the human being is φῦσει ἀναμάρτητον [*physei anamartēton:* "sinless by nature"]. Does this mean that one does not sin? Obviously not. How then *does* one sin? Because the sins for which one can be guilty must result from wrong choices freely made, it is crucial that a person's *nature* be carefully distinguished from his *choices.* In turn, while the choice to do good always rests with us, the *accomplishment* of good choices comes only by way of συνεργεία [*synergeia:* "cooperation"] with God. Wrong choices — evil — are made *without* God's cooperation, leaving him free to abandon us justly.[39]

In summary, three cardinal points in the Eastern Christian tradition about human nature and decision-making stand in contrast with modern Western approaches. This tradition holds that (1) human beings are born with a freedom given along with the image of God; (2) human beings sin by the choices they make whenever these choices contradict what they "by nature" were meant to be — sinless; and (3) human beings are promised newness of life — transformation, forgiveness, and restoration — whenever they freely make rectifying choices in cooperation with God. Such views contrast with the popular Western notion, rooted in Augustinian theology, that to be human and to be sinful are virtually the same thing. If the fact that in God's image we were originally created "very good" (Gen. 1.31) is denied, it becomes nearly impossible to separate the person of the sinner from the sin that he commits. The sinner is thus forced to commit "self-hatred" — something which St. Paul says is impossible (Eph. 5.29), and which ultimately led into the state of ἀκηδία [*akēdia:* "despair"], a spiritual state that was

38. *Ibid.,* 320.
39. *Ibid.,* 262.

gravely warned against by the elders. When this condition regresses to self-loathing, it is at least as debilitating to the Christian life as are arrogance and pride.

Many contemporary schools of thought advise people to accept as "natural" a condition which is, truthfully, *inhuman.* The Eastern Christian understanding of human nature, in confirming its basic goodness, counters the typical excuse that when we sin we are "only being human,"with the assertion that when we sin we are, in fact, not being *human enough*! Sinfulness is *unnatural* for us, and man's willful fall into sin did not end God's approval of humanity per se. the Incarnation is the mark of that approval, for Christ could not have put on something innately sinful.

Through his application of this theology to the concrete, everyday tales of improper choices made by his directees, the spiritual director is a positive agent of growth, used by God to affirm their natural goodness, despite their acts. His task is to guide and counsel people as to how they can overcome what is unnatural, and thus to realize eveything that is natural and good. What a person says will be conditioned by the predicament in which he finds him- or herself. Many are tyrannized and held in bondage by the Devil himself, others by the various "gods" of our day — sociological, psychological, cultural, even those of religion gone awry. The desires of the body and the demands of such ideologies on the mind seek to capture our attention, and in so doing debilitate our Christian life. We often are radically un-free — and thereby, also inhuman. It is not difficult to see why we might wish to hide like Adam. But the prospect of being truly set free, of living in harmony with our true nature, should also draw us out of hiding and lead us to make a free decision to love God with our whole being and our neighbor as ourself (Mk. 12.30-31). The *inner way* is a continual effort to make this rectifying choice and to be healed.

## 5. Between the Therapeutic and Theological: The Place of Metaphorical Language

Our fifth "spiritual" concern is with the relationship between the therapeutic and the theological, both of which are involved in the healing process of spiritual direction. Experience, as we have seen above, is a *locus theologicus* — an avenue by which God enters human life to effect restoration, reconciliation, growth, etc. Healing is the heart of spiritual direction, and so must take advantage of all the tools available. Seminary professor Thomas Hart offers a helpful perspective:

> Our training is often of minimal help. Those of us who teach theology usually know little of counseling, and so, of course, do not speak of it. Those of us who teach counseling care little for theology, and never advert to it. . . . The art that still eludes many of us is that of a smooth integration of these two perspectives, *the therapeutic and the theological,* so that both are fully operative in the work we do.[40]

How can the therapeutic and theological both be put to work in a united *praxis?* Selecting appropriate *language* in spiritual direction seems a likely place to start in overcoming the traditionally uneasy alliance between the two. At the outset we can recall that no matter how the term "therapist" has evolved in modern, colloquial usage, its origins rest in the term θεράπων [*therapōn:* "Godly servant"],[41] and that historically the healing performed in spiritual direction was often referred to as θεραπεία Θεοῦ [*therapeia Theou:* "the therapy of God"]. As such godly therapy was also Our Lord's primary task, we can profitably examine his methods and his use of language.

Jesus made use of illustrations, examples, and narratives in talking to the people, but his primary means of conveying a lesson was the parable (παραβολή [*parabolē*]).[42] His example was followed in the literature of the *Apophthegmata Patrum,* with its plethora of stories and "sayings." From Christ's own words down through the example of the "compost heap," the *metaphor* runs as a constant thread through Christian literature.

"Metaphor" is a combination of μετά [*meta:* "over"] and φορά [*phora:* "carrying"]; it should, therefore, prove a most natural form for "carrying over" crucial lessons to directees — and providing a common interface for theology and therapy. As Sallie McFague defines it:

40. Thomas Hart, "Counseling's Spiritual Dimension," *Journal of Pastoral Care* 43.2 (1989), 111.

41. This term is explained in "The Being in Act of Theology," in Joseph J. Allen, ed., *Orthodox Synthesis* (Crestwood, NY: St. Vladimir's Seminary Press, 1981), 104-5.

42. See "Story in the Old and New Testament," in Allen, *Ministry,* 165-69.

> Most simply, a metaphor is seeing one thing *as* something else, pretending "this" is "that," because we do not know how to think or talk about "this," and so we use "that" as a way of saying something about it. Thinking metaphorically means spotting a thread of similarity between two dissimilar objects, events, or whatever, one of which is better known than the other, and using the better-known one as a way of speaking about the lesser known.[43]

When she goes on to point out that "as a form of religious language, the parables (a metaphorical form of language) in the New Testament, are very different from [other] symbolic, sacramental language,"[44] she offers a valuable insight into how language can serve the endeavor of healing. As scripture itself demonstrates, the metaphor does not have to assume from the outset a believing or religious perspective on the part of the listener. Indeed, it does not assume any continuity between our world and the transcendent one, between the ways of this world and those of God.

> On the contrary, they — metaphors — are a secular form of language, telling stories of ordinary people in mundane family, business, and social matters; they assume a discontinuity between our ways and the ways of the Kingdom.[45]

How, then, can God enter through them? If in spiritual direction the directee speaks in a "secular form of language," telling stories of ordinary people — as well he or she might — and the director also adopts such a form of language, this does not necessarily mean that God is absent from the experience; in fact, he will *not* be absent if metaphors are properly utilized.

McFague describes precisely what Our Lord accomplished through his use of parables. Speaking about love, compassion, joy, hope, etc. — various avenues of healing and restoration in everyday life — Jesus also communicated the transcendent message of God's healing presence (or absence, as the case may be). Can metaphor provide a common language for therapy and theology — one with sufficient power to bring about

43. *Metaphorical Theology: Models of God in Religious Language* (Philadelphia: Fortress, 1988), 15.

44. *Ibid.*, 14.

45. *Ibid.*, 15.

healing? Oliver Morgan presents a number of scenarios which seem to demonstrate that indeed it can.

Morgan contextualizes his use of metaphor by the declaration that "spirituality is a way of living in explicit relation to God and neighbor," and that the human experience, through listening, discerning, and taking responsible action, can nourish this way of life. "Spirituality is a vital union of spiritual experience, vision, and praxis," he states.[46] Indeed, metaphorical language "is a way in which we can articulate an experience and comprehension of ourselves, others, and God."[47] Moreover, every person intuitively turns to this form of language in the search for that self-understanding which leads to self-transcendence:

> Each of us utilizes metaphors for the articulation and deep appropriation of our experiences and their meanings. . . . Metaphors reveal, and offer the potential to re-interpret, our ways of being and acting in the world. They offer a path for seeing linkages in who we are, what we do, and how we do it.[48]

Morgan offers two useful examples. Inside a mental hospital, a young man is bound in a strait-jacket, sitting in a large, dark room. Isolated and alone, cut off from any human companionship and confused in his perceptions, he is unkempt, unshaven, and wild-eyed. "Stresses, frustrations, terrors seem to be assaulting him from within, and he feels defenseless before the onslaught." He realizes, however, that he has not always been like this; the lack of clarity and cloudiness which so frighten him have not always been present. "He feels beset, overmatched, defeated. 'Who will rescue me from the pit?'"

The second example involves a medical hospital, with an accident victim its major player. "He is paralyzed from the neck down . . . [and] cannot see beyond vague distortions" as he struggles to break through his bandages. "When he rises above the stupor of shock and medications, he is aware of feeling cut-off, out-of-touch, disoriented." In his more lucid moments, the victim amidst loneliness and fear wonders what could possibly bring light into his darkness. "Who can save me in this time of trouble?" He wonders about hope — "until someone grasps his

46. Oliver Morgan, "Elements in a Spirituality of Pastoral Care," *Journal of Pastoral Care* 43.2 (1989), 99.

47. *Ibid.*

48. *Ibid.*

hand! This he can feel. This sudden connection has strength, resolve, and compassion in it. He feels flooded with hope and love."[49]

Morgan then comments on the impact that these stories had on him:

> These two metaphors acted as lenses. . . . They aided me in seeing the alienation and isolation that are part of illness and sin. They functioned as indicators of inner estrangement and disorientation, catching the essential neediness that can arise from one's *own* wounds and sins. . . . They became central, organizing metaphors for motivation and involvement in a "healing ministry."[50]

Such metaphors provided him the stuff of "memories, affects, and understandings" which he subsequently put to use in the course of healing. Is this not also the function, for example, of the parable of the Good Samaritan? Could it not also prove a means of creating a "linkage" between the "everyday, normal experiences" which directees bring into the dialogue of spiritual direction, and which provide no healing power simply because they do not incorporate the action of God within them? Through the use of metaphors, the director can offer hope.

More particularly, the director can encourage a person to *be* and *act* metaphorically as he or she looks back over the events of a lifetime. The directee can be guided to reflect on memories of those individuals who influenced his or her life, and perhaps draw out the message of hope that they bore through courageous responses to particular predicaments. Their words, causes, and behavior can become guideposts to follow, catalysts for change, which, in turn, would naturally lead to an increased sense of self-worth and commitment on the part of the directee. With such increased potential, the person can be helped to face future trials with the kind of Christian hope and integrity which he or she remembers displayed by that revered person from the past.

However, we need not limit our use of such guiding metaphors to the individuals that populate a directee's personal past. We can — and should — draw on the great heroes of scripture, literature, and history. This is one of the most important functions of the study of *hagiography* (the study of great saints) for promoting personal faith. Contact with exemplary persons can function in a metaphorical way for the one

49. *Ibid.*, 100-101.
50. *Ibid.*

struggling in the present. Their stories suggest ways by which we might walk through our own stories, even though they will not be identical.

> Their life stories function as "guiding metaphors" for us, revealing and interpreting some of the mysteries of our lives, grounding and articulating some of the dreams which help to form us as persons. In the way of metaphor, our familiarity with aspects of *their* story helps to illuminate the unfamiliarity of *our* selves, *our* stories.[51]

Thus there are two lessons about the language of metaphor which the spiritual director can use in his ministry. First, he can introduce various stories and parables from scripture, general literature, even his own life, for the directee to meditate upon. These should be carefully selected to illustrate that the directee is not alone, that the present experience has, in a sense, *already* occurred, and that at least one example exists of a person he or she can admire having walked through a similar valley in his or her own life.

Second, since each of us has been, in one way or another, touched positively or negatively by past relationships, the directee can be led to understand the influences and impact of individuals from his own past. There is certainly enough evidence on disfunctional family systems to show how relationships impact on each of the persons involved. It is important to realize that these relationships do not *remain buried* in the past; they continue to influence and press in on the directee's judgments long afterward, and the director can utilize these experiences to help promote present healing by learning to "listen" to metaphorical memories.

Every mundane experience can thus provide the forum for healing from God. The language need not be "religious" or "spiritual" per se. Many of Our Lord's parables demonstrate this truth, for like those of Oliver Morgan, they speak of simple experiences which are at once therapeutic and theological.

51. *Ibid.*, 106.

## 6. Compassion, Steadfast Love, Faithfulness: Correlates for Healing

Our sixth theological concern continues the examination of therapy and theology by seeking to determine the proper place in spiritual direction of the qualities of *compassion, steadfast love,* and *faithfulness* in the healer. Such virtues were considered obligatory in the elder. He was instructed, in fact, to remain in touch with his own experiences of suffering, sinfulness, and limitations precisely in order always to manifest these virtues to his directees. By cultivating these qualities through struggling with his own inner experiences, the elder found himself able to offer guidance and counsel to others.

These three "theologically-rooted" qualities of ministry, which can be seen at work in Our Lord's own care for a broken world, closely correlate with the "therapeutic" qualities of *empathy, holding environment,* and *alliance;* their closeness suggests another link between the "spiritual" and "direction" components of the healing process. Morgan warns us to make this connection cautiously, however:

> I am not proposing here a one-to-one correspondence between these religious and clinical terms. Complex nuances and linguistic contexts inform and contextualize each of them. Rather, I am suggesting a softer kind of correlation, a more general stance, an attitude of persons.[52]

What is the nature of this proposed correlation, and how is healing realized through it? In theology, *compassion* means that the sufferer is "grasped" by one who "co-passionates." The directee realizes that his or her director, because he is in vital touch with his own experience of pain, loss, and sinfulness, is truly "walking with him"; the directee knows him- or herself to be a "loved sinner," who, even if his sin is hated, is nevertheless loved by a "wounded healer" and "fellow pilgrim." In therapy, *empathy* helps healing to occur because the patient feels that his or her counselor is truly capable of entering his frame and perspective; "he

52. *Ibid.,* 103. The author, in the section entitled "Sensibility and Pastoral Relationship," uses the correlations *compassion/empathy, steadfast love/holding environment, faithfulness/therapeutic alliance,* in endeavoring to show that within the experiential environment, "spirituality" is able to correlate theology-based and therapeutics-based qualities within the ministry of healing. The religious and clinical terms, he claims, are not easily separated, since both speak at once of the healing process.

can see from where I see." Sharon Parks claims that empathy is the ability to "love tenderly . . . with an awareness of the capacity of the other to be wounded, to suffer pain, and to be dependent upon relationships with others."[53] This correlation is clear.

The second theological quality is *steadfast love,* a reflection of God's *hesed.* He unshakably loves a people that is sinful and suffering. He understands both our vulnerabilities and our potential. He is at once both tender and tenacious in his love.[54] Theologically, we can know that God will remain utterly steadfast in his love, will not desert or abandon us — even if we "strive" with him in the manner of Jacob at the brook of Jabbok (Gen. 32.24-32). The therapeutic correlate of steadfast love is known as the *"holding environment."* It promotes healing by creating a context or atmosphere of nurture and support within the dialogue. This atmosphere "holds together" the patient and counselor through the former's troubling predicament. "Such a holding environment is essential for the reconstruction, which is the goal of pastoral therapeutics."[55] The nature of this supportive environment is to "hold on" — to provide steadfastness — despite all the potential strife in the environment. James Fowler speaks of this same phenomenon as "reconstructive change" in the face of failure, and claims that the movement toward it requires an "ecology of care and vocation," in order for the passage from old to new to be successful.[56]

The third theological quality is *faithfulness.* God is unshakably faithful to his unworthy people. For the Christian, there are two clear demonstrations of God's faithfulness: Jesus Christ as the Incarnation of God's faithful Word and Promise, and the presence of the Holy Spirit who is sent to abide as Advocate and Comforter. The therapeutic correlate suggested by Nagy and Krasner[57] is *alliance,* meaning a trustworthiness on the part of the counselor, a relational presence and intervention. The patient knows that his counselor will not suddenly abandon — or "let go of" — this alliance, will not suddenly release the grip that they have shared. This confidence provides an indispensable element in healing.

53. Walter Brueggemann, Sharon Parks, and Thomas H. Groome, *To Act Justly, Love Tenderly, Walk Humbly: An Agenda for Ministers* (New York: Paulist Press, 1986), 30.

54. *Ibid.,* 39.

55. Morgan, "Elements," 104.

56. James Fowler, *Faith Development and Pastoral Care* (Philadelphia: Fortress, 1987), 103-6.

57. Ivan Nagy and Barbara Krasner, "Trust-based Therapy: A Contextual Approach," *American Journal of Psychiatry* 137 (1980), 767-75.

It is important for contemporary spiritual direction that we understand these theological/therapeutic correlations, for they help us appreciate how healing can be rooted in theology and yet adopt a psychological methodology. The possibility and advisability of binding together seemingly diverse elements is beginning to emerge.

### 7. The Binding of the "Spiritual" and the "Direction"

In our study of the *inner way,* it is critical to understand how the two components, "spiritual" and "direction," are bound together. The way has been prepared by our investigation of the integration of therapy and theology through the correlation of terminology, and in the use of metaphorical language to "carry over" healing messages. But for "spiritual" and "direction" to be truly bound, we must understand the fundamental issues of a proper Christian anthropology.

The Eastern Christian tradition looks at humankind in an all-encompassing and comprehensive way. Our theology informs not only our self-perception but our interpersonal relations, our communal life and organization, and our acknowledgment of the self-worth of every human being created in God's image. In the Old Testament we read, "Then God said, 'Let us make humankind in our image, according to our likeness . . .'" (Gen. 1.26). . ." and St. Paul comments in the New: "Do not lie to one another, seeing that you have stripped off the old self with its practices and have clothed yourselves with the new self, which is being renewed in knowledge according to the image of its creator" (Col. 3.9-10).

This "theology of the image" is the veritable starting point for all theological investigation, the dogmatic pillar for all anthropological reflection. In the fourteenth century, St. Nicholas Cabasilas used it to explain the Incarnation:

> He it was who came to earth and retrieved his own Image, and he came to a place where the sheep was straying and lifted it up and stopped it from straying.[58]

58. St. Nicholas Cabasilas, *The Life in Christ,* trans. Carmino J. Decantazaro (Crestwood, NY: St. Vladimir's Seminary Press, 1974), 50.

The "theology of the image" also arms one for battle in a spiritual direction, for it allows the human being — through God's grace and his or her own free will — to choose and respond, and hence to grow continually into communion with God. Life is never static. We are always growing into communion with God ("*theosis*": God-likeness) when we make right choices, or falling away from him when we make wrong ones.[59]

Thomas Hart, a practicing spiritual director, helps us "see the spiritual dimension operating in the situations of people who come to us with their problems, and how to work with that dimension in therapy."[60] By doing so, Hart can help us better to appreciate the importance of the "theology of the image," to find how to bind together the spiritual and direction components, and thus to solidify our understanding of how theology and therapy are integrated in the healing practice. His nine "guiding principles" present a picture of Christian anthropology in which the theological roots of spiritual direction are obvious. We will investigate the seven which I think most relevant to our present task, applying our distinctively Eastern theological understandings to each: the spiritual director must be firmly grounded in — and work out of — sound theology; otherwise his work differs little from that of the secular counselor.

In one form or another, each of Hart's principles speaks about how the Christian is to understand theologically who is the human being. Who is God? What does it mean that we are created in his image? What happens to our relationship with God and others when we make choices? How do we grow into deeper communion? How do we grow away from God? How does God penetrate our lives? These questions — and others like them — are truly "theological," and provide the anthropological context in which a spiritual director can go about guiding and counseling his directees.

59. See *St. Athanasius on the Incarnation: The Treatise De Incarnatione Verbi Dei*, translated by a Religious of C.S.M.V. (Crestwood, NY: St. Vladimir's Seminary Press, 1953), 28-29. There are also many commentaries; e.g.: Vladimir Lossky, *Orthodox Theology: An Introduction* (Crestwood, NY: St. Vladimir's Seminary Press, 1978), 71-72; Fr. Georges Florovsky, "Creation and Creaturehood," in *Creator and Redemption (Collected Works of Georges Florovsky,* 3) (Belmont, MA: Nordland Publishing, 1978), 74ff.; and Fr. John Meyendorff, *Christ in Eastern Christian Thought,* 3d ed. (Crestwood, NY: St. Vladimir's Seminary Press, 1975), 147ff.

60. Thomas Hart, "Nine Guiding Principles," *Journal of Pastoral Care* 43.2 (1989), 111-18.

*a. God is the depth-dimension of all experiences.*

This principle presumes that God is real. Its importance lies in pointing to where God is. God *made* us and somehow guides the course of our world. We are ultimately responsible to him. As we have seen, in the biblical tradition this transcendent mystery is variously symbolized in evocative metaphors drawn from human experience. Whatever the symbolic presentation of God in any given book or passage, there runs through scripture a conviction based on a people's religious experience that this mysterious source of all things is personal and benevolent toward us, and furthermore, is in some sort of dialogue with each of us. We can, therefore, in spiritual direction assume that God is *already* present in the lives we direct — no matter how aware or unaware the directees may be of this as they begin to unfold their stories.

*b. Where the action in a person's life is,*
*God is most present and active.*

Although spiritual direction is not based upon crises, it is nevertheless the crisis situation that more often than not brings people for direction in the first place. Someone has died. An illicit affair has developed. A teenager has grown unbearably hard to deal with. Addiction has gained a grip. Oppression or loneliness has turned life into an intolerable burden. One way or another the "compost heap" stands ready to be turned over, and God can be most present and active in the lives of those involved. The questions we must ask include: "What is God's call in these circumstances?" "What challenges and opportunities does this situation offer?" "To what healing or growth is God inviting us?" A person must reflect on each of these questions as his or her story unfolds. As the director and directee discuss together what is happening, each will probably have something to contribute, as gradually they clarify the situation over time.

*c. God wants life for us.*

The spiritual director must constantly recall that God is our ally and friend. The human project is God's project. Life is God's gift, and his purpose in giving it was that it be lived *properly.* Wherever healing, liberation, and growth are taking place, God's purpose is truly being realized. Where people are finding one another in true love and reaching their greatest possible fulfillment, God's activity is achieving its goal. God stands against all that oppresses, limits, and causes pain. He labors *with* us — but not in place of us — for liberation, healing, reconciliation, harmony, and joy. The director must counsel that evil also exists in the world, because human freedom also exists — and often goes astray, producing destruction. He must remind the directee that when our loved ones are in pain, it is not the pain but *life* which God desires for them. They can be confident that God is already at work *with them* on the side of all that will promote their liberation, healing, and growth, and *against* everything that is allied with evil and affliction. God is there to help them draw out of their situation all the good that can possibly be drawn out. And when as spiritual directors we guide others to these same ends, we are collaborating with God's own work.

### *d. God does not send us tragedy and suffering, but works with us in them for good.*

This principle is a logical consequence of the preceding one, and is drawn out explicitly only because it is so vitally important for dealing with the various sufferings of human life. The director must teach that it was *not* God who willed or caused our sexual abuse as children; it is *not* God who sends us cancer or AIDS; it is *not* God who brought about our divorce, willed us to be lonely, or decided to plunge us into poverty (see 2 Pet. 3.8-9 and Jas. 1.13). Where, then, *is* God with respect to these conditions that affect us so profoundly? First, he is grieving with us in our pain. Second, he is working with us to bring forth all possible good from the evil we are suffering. God stands *with* us rather than against us. The tragedies of our lives are precisely what God did *not* want to happen; he wants life for us. But now that they have come our way, he stands with us in our grief and he attends our struggle, to work with us to bring from them all the good that can be realized.

*e. The proper Christian response to suffering is to resist and try to overcome it, only then accepting the unsolved remainder in hope.*

In both the Old and New Testaments God works consistently to free people from the sufferings that oppress them. Jesus, in God's name, labored to alleviate human pain; he even prayed that his own appointed suffering might pass him by, only then accepting it and entrusting his cause to his Father. Suffering is not good *in itself,* and the spiritual response to it should be the same as the instinctive one: to strive to remove it. However, when we have done all we *can* do, but the suffering is still there, *hope* still remains because, as we have seen, God works with us in our sufferings to bring whatever good can be brought out of them beyond this earthly life.

There is in spiritual direction a temptation to put the second part of the principle before the first — to make it appear that suffering is always a good thing because good can come of it. Some even elevate suffering to a sign of God's special favor. Although there is a venerable tradition to this teaching, Jesus never said to a person who was hurting, "This is good for you" or "This is God's will for you" or "This is a mark of God's special love." Wherever he saw pain he moved directly and promptly to relieve it. In like manner, this should be our first motivation in the face of suffering.

Second, we must view *depression* as an obvious evil, and as far as possible overcome it, since it militates against hope. Relationships that tear us down are always evil and should be recognized as such. Much of the "spiritual" opportunity and invitation in these situations lies *not* in some fainthearted response, but in striving to overcome them. Only when we have done all that we can do, does the opportunity arise for personal growth by accepting the sufferings. In any case, a Christian must never lose that hope by which he is to be "anchored" (1 Pet. 1.3).

*f. When we have determined what we most deeply want, we have found what God wants for us.*

This is perhaps the boldest of Hart's principles and the most likely to raise quick doubt. What does *my* will have to do with God's? They seem at first glance totally unrelated — quite possibly even opposed. Indeed, they may be opposites, and the spiritual director must be aware of this. However, this principle speaks not of any want I might have, but of my *deepest* want! The kind of wanting envisioned here is spiritually reasoned and mature, a product of both mind and heart, a desire at my very center that persists over time. It has little to do with sudden impulses or transitory whims. Its language is not "I feel like . . ." or "Sometimes I think I'd like. . . ." This principle is based on the basic Christian presupposition that a person's life is basically oriented toward good, toward communion with God. This does not mean that a person never does anything wrong, but only that the basic orientation of his or her life is toward what is true and good. One takes one's lapses *seriously* and genuinely regrets them, but what one *habitually* seeks to discover and do is that which is true and good.

### *g. It is true love that we are made for: love for God, others, and self.*

Love is the Christian meaning of our lives. We find our fulfillment in giving and receiving it. Nothing else will do. This is not false love — loving the wrong things. True loving is loving correctly. It takes a long time to love others well. It is perhaps equally difficult to receive love from others, to believe in it, to accept it, and to let it nourish us. Nor does it come easily to many of us genuinely to love (and respect) ourselves. For the spiritual director, therefore, love presents the problem of an open-ended prospect of growth over a lifetime. Love is the core spiritual issue of our humanity.

Every therapeutic issue in spiritual direction comes down in some way or another to *love*, the kind of love known in the scriptures as ἀγάπη [*agapē*]. "God is love" (1 Jn. 4.8), and we are made in God's image. Many who seek a spiritual director have very low self-esteem. Many hate rather than love themselves. Others feel that their lives are meaningless and empty. The problem is often that they do not love anyone *else* and are not giving anything to anyone else. It is no wonder that their lives are empty, when so much of our satisfaction as human beings created in God's image derives from giving to others.

Love is never a simple matter, and this makes it very difficult to discuss in spiritual direction. We have to struggle to figure out how to love another person well. Much of the marital struggle lies in learning how to love just this one mysterious person well. Children present a similar challenge — each one of them individually. In their case it is particularly clear that genuine Christian love is not always best expressed by giving them everything they claim to want. When we examine what is really best for them, we might well find ourselves expressing love by saying "No."

Despite all its potential aberrations, love is central to human life and central to Christian theology — and as such becomes a central concern in therapy. The spiritual director's eye of discernment must certainly remain peeled to assure that the conditions for love are properly expressed.

To summarize, then, in the words of Thomas Hart:

> It is hoped that this articulation will help us . . . to move back and forth . . . between the realms of therapy and theology. Most people who come to us want and need quality in both areas. Fortunately, the thrust of good therapy and the thrust of good theology converge on a common goal: the healing, liberation, and growth of the human being.[61]

## 8. Caring and Curing: Listening, Affirming, Freeing

> From experience you know that those who *care* for you become present to you. When they speak, they speak to *you.* And when they ask questions, you know it is for *your* sake and not their own. Their presence is a healing presence, because they accept you on your terms, and they encourage you to take you own life seriously and to trust your own vocation.[62]

In this healing relationship it is less important that a "cure" be found — that an ending point be reached — than that "care" be given — that a ministry of compassion be engaged. This is obvious in the Gospel narratives, where Jesus' healing ministry springs from the fact that he is "moved with compassion": καὶ ἐσπλαγχνίσθη ἐπ' αὐτοῖς [*kai es-*

61. *Ibid.,* 118.

62. Henri Nouwen, *Out of Solitude* (Notre Dame, IN: Notre Dame Press, 1974), 36.

*planchnisthē ep' autois:* "And he had compassion on them"] (Mk. 6.34; see also Mt. 20.34 and Lk. 7.13, *inter alia*). The root in Greek, σπλάγχνον [*splanchnon*] designates the inner parts, the viscera, identified figuratively in the Old Testament as the "bowels of compassion." In the passage which opened our discussion of this eighth theological concern, Henri Nouwen emphasizes that a healing relationship can require physical movement — a "going out" to another in his or her time of need, responding with a touch, a gesture, a life-giving word. Such caring goes far beyond vague and superficial emotions, or a general concession that somebody "needs help." It is a liberating movement which reveals to the one who suffers his or her own worth, and the inward capacity to become what he or she was created to be. Such is the fruit of a healing relationship which is marked by true care.

A person feels accepted when first he learns that he is "acceptable." This is a crucial theological lesson. It is fully described in the story of the woman taken in adultery (Jn. 8.1-11), in Jesus' attitude and response. To accept oneself is not to *settle* for oneself. We must distinguish between acceptance and approval. Only when a person truly comes to accept him- or herself — often after learning from some other significant person that he or she is considered "acceptable" — can he enact his own commitment to further growth, to the possibility of positive change.

Helping a person undertake such growth and change is difficult and challenging. Mixed in with the "reachable" options open to each of us are innumerable grandiose goals and unrealistic projects for which we are too limited, but to which we are drawn by our own will. We ourselves — and those who truly care about us — must ask, "What is realistically possible and what is not?" "Are there shortcomings with which we must simply come to terms and which then must be left alone, as 'tares among the wheat' that must be allowed to grow?" (see Mt. 13.24-43). "Is there 'a thorn in the flesh' — a persistent personal demon — which must continue to abide and buffet?" (2 Cor. 12.7-9). Together spiritual director and directee must realize with St. Paul that the grace of Christ, and his victory over corruption and sin, provides hope beyond the immediate. There is grace even within the handicaps that we are asked to bear. Through a ministry of compassionate care, the spiritual director can bring his directee to the point of self-acceptance. Healing requires a synthesis of *patience* which encompasses endurance and humility, and of *hope* in the lordship of Jesus and the power of the Spirit.

Jacques Pasquier claims that there are three theological elements necessary in any healing relationship, and which are particularly applicable to the caring aspect of this process. These are *listening, affirming,* and *freeing.*[63] Every person wants to communicate in a trusting relationship, "and yet we experience over and over again that nobody listens to us."

> Why is it that we see and hear the same people repeat the same complaints, the same stories, for months and years? For the simple reason that they have never been heard. Whether their stories are objectively true or not is irrelevant. The point is that as long as a person has not experienced what it means to be heard by another, *he will either withdraw or become more and more aggressive.* . . . The more he experiences this feeling of not being heard, the more he strives to protect himself behind the walls of his own making.[64]

This is an important point. The person who reaches out for another to listen is often lonely and determined to rid him- or herself of that loneliness. Frustration forces him to project a variety of masks, facades, and personae to hide the hurt. To those with "eyes to see, ears to hear, and a heart to perceive" such tactics not only fail to hide the truth, but in fact make it blatantly obvious.

What can be done? How is the spiritual director to respond? "The first step in the healing process is when the pain is truly perceived," Pasquier declares: "This is what listening is all about."[65] The spiritual director must listen in such a way as to appreciate and perceive the *real* content of what is being said — the pain behind the words, the fear behind the aggression, the insecurity behind the rigidity, the guilt behind the compensation. In order to convey to the directee the feeling of acceptance which can lead to his or her own self-acceptance, the director must at first listen without judging, evaluating, or minimizing what is said. Jesus said nothing to the adulterous woman until all had had their say. He listened quietly to *everything* — the Pharisees' angry shouts, the woman's guilt- and fear-ridden silence. And then he accepted her in order for the healing transformation to begin.

Why is it so difficult truly to listen? Why is it so difficult to care

63. Jacques Pasquier, "Healing Relationships," *The Way* (1976), 208-16.
64. *Ibid.*, 212-13.
65. *Ibid.*

enough to listen? "Essentially because we are afraid of what we will hear, afraid of being confronted with a hurt to which we would not be able to respond."[66] We do not listen because we're looking out for "Number One." We are too self-protective to care. The spiritual director in particular must realize that he does not have to have an immediate word of "cure" in order to be an agent of "care." He must drop his self-image as all-knowing "messiah," and, like his suffering directee, accept that sometimes it is in our own powerlessness that God's healing power is made known (2 Cor. 12.9).

The second element in caring is *affirmation.* For its meaning we return to the Gospel of John where we can note Jesus' precise words to the adulterous woman: "Neither do I condemn you." He hears her guilt, her shame, her fear, but he affirms that she has within herself the power given by God to accept herself, her responsibility, her possibilities, and — yes — even her sinfulness. "To affirm is to say 'yes' *to whom the person is:* to recognize that there is in each person the power of self-reconciliation, of growth, of becoming whole again."[67] We must never forget that while healing can only proceed from within a person, from the reservoir of his or her inner power, the *source* of healing is God's own grace which is given by the Holy Spirit (Rom. 5.5). One's inner person — his or her depths — serves as a conduit for the flow of God's grace. Often the process becomes activated only after the person finds affirmation by an external "other" (in this case the spiritual director), but then he or she is able to let the true inner person express itself with the full activity of the conscience. In seeking to affirm the directee, the director must be careful not to provide crutches for the lame, but boldly to say, "Get up and walk!" He must believe that, with proper care, the directee will find the power within to make the correct choices, and thus to become a co-creator with the ultimate Creator in whose image he or she is shaped.

The third element is *freedom* or liberty — St. Paul's beloved ἐλευθερία [*eleutheria*]. In spiritual direction freedom must be viewed as a *process* rather than a final product. Once one has gained freedom from internal bonds (whatever they may be), he or she is not absolutely free, but has only begun the process of becoming free. We use the word "becoming" intentionally, in the sense of an ongoing mission, a continual unfolding and growth. When Jesus forgives and heals, it is also

66. *Ibid.*, 213.
67. *Ibid.*

the beginning of a process: "Go and sin no more" or "Go in peace" or "Go, your faith has saved you" (Jn. 8.11 and Lk. 7.50, *inter alia*).

This is an important theological lesson for true care in spiritual direction. Freedom is realized in forgiveness. But forgiveness is possible only when one has freely decided to be vulnerable to God's continuing self-revelation — that he is love and that his love can free us. Thus, to be free is to say "yes" to God — but also to oneself. This does not require or demonstrate pride or arrogance; it simply acknowledges that even though, by all standards, one is radically *un*-acceptable, God nevertheless loves and accepts him or her. "No one has condemned you . . . neither do I condemn you," said Jesus to the woman; these are his caring words — all at once — of forgiveness, acceptance, and freedom. When a person knows that God has forgiven him, then he can forgive himself. God's forgiveness must lead to self-forgiveness, not vice versa. Of course, the spiritual director's job is to see that the flow is in the proper direction.[68]

Listening, affirming, and freeing. All three of these theologically-rooted elements are necessary in spiritual direction if it is to be focused on "care" rather than "cure." The spiritual director must utilize them in such a way as to help the directee make correct choices on his own, and not to remove from him his God-given freedom of choice. The person must be made to accept accountability for his freedom, and thus the responsibility for growing toward God.

> The freedom to be — and to become — what we are, is possible only when we experience that we no longer need to be constantly self-protective by hiding behind walls, facades, roles. In the whole mystery of death and life, what I am afraid of is not so much the "death" part, as the "life" part: because it calls me to be more than what I am; and that can be very threatening indeed.[69]

Only if we truly care can we communicate to another that he or she is chosen, loved, and named by God, and therefore a free and responsible

68. Of course, in the end one can never truly "forgive oneself." By definition, this is impossible, since forgiveness always needs an external "other" in order to be efficacious. The phrase "to forgive oneself," rather, means that one accepts into oneself — internalizes, fully receives — God's forgiveness. It is a phrase which makes sense only because many people have great difficulty in accepting forgiveness, and therefore must "learn to forgive themselves."

69. Pasquier, "Healing," 215.

co-creator with God the Creator. Care is really the key to the healing relationship found on the *inner way.*

## 9. The Place of the Heart

Examining the "place of the heart"[70] is a fitting way to conclude our look at the "spiritual" component in spiritual direction. In Eastern Christian theology the heart is the primary location for communion, healing, growth, reconciliation — and more. There God and human beings meet in the experiences of the covenantal life (see Mt. 5.8, Mk. 7.21-23, Rom. 6.17, Jas. 4.8, and a multitude of Old Testament sources). There we make our free-will choices, as St. John of Damascus so clearly showed. There we struggle. There we pray. There the deepest efforts in spiritual direction occur. There we confront the everyday — every-minute — predicaments of life. There we find the wide range of impediments to proper Christian living: the "breakdowns" within individuals and between people — spouses, in-laws, co-workers. There reside the perceptions which color how we will behave toward others. Earlier we spoke about the depths out of which one cries — the vast reservoir of both good and evil within us. Those depths and the heart are one. The heart is that spiritual place where both healing and sin reside.

If the heart is all of this, then it is there that the spiritual director must apply all that he has learned from history and theology. He must earn our trust in order to gain access to our heart. He must help us find the courage to reveal all the sins which hide therein. He must help us "die" there, in order to be reborn. He must walk with us there, listening to all we say, guiding us to understand our own intentions behind the words. He must help us sweep away any "idols" we have set up there, come to grips with ourselves and cooperate with God's grace — which also dwells within our hearts. With gentleness, firmness, and love he

70. I have intentionally used the phrase "*place* of the heart" since I do not want merely to project an image of the physical organ of the heart and circulatory system. There is a plethora of Eastern Christian literature explaining the use of the term as the "seat of one's deepest being," or, as noted earlier, one's spiritual "depths." There are, of course, some theories which purport to show the connection between the heart as a spiritual place and the physical organ, as, for example, when one dies "of a broken heart." I do not want, however, to emphasize this here.

must help us reorder the self-image which we hold within, confront false pride, grand eloquence, and defeatism; he must help us realize that, as Daniel Williams says, "the self-image is never *only* a self-image."[71] He must help us see the discrepancy between what we are, what we pretend to be, and what we really ought to be.

We as directees can respond on one of three levels: *insight, behavior,* or *being.* William Oglesby writes about these:

> It is evident that all three are genuinely concerned with 'right-knowing' (*insight*-orientation), 'right-doing' (*behavior*-orientation), and 'right-being' (*personal* transformation) . . . [and] that all three concepts are important. Indeed, there is a sense in which the whole story of God's revelation and human response can be told in terms of knowing, doing, and being. The crucial question . . . is which of these is seen as primary and which derivative?[72]

In spiritual direction and Eastern Christian theology generally — and in our present context specifically — "right-being" is given priority. This is yet another way of describing the "place of the heart." From right-being emerge both "right-knowing" and "right-doing," whose limitations are clear. Oglesby concurs: neither "insight" nor "doing" can be an end in itself. Neither goes far enough.

Whereas most secular therapists can content themselves with "insight," and the behaviorists end at "doing," the spiritual director's target in guiding those entrusted to his care must be "right-being" — the "place of the heart." If conversion, reconciliation, and transformation are to occur in a person, then he or she must experience nothing short of a "change of heart." The directee must be guided into the heart, no matter how painful the process might be, for spiritual growth can occur in no other way. Certainly the spiritual director will not overlook or ignore the first two levels, but he will not stop short of his ultimate goal. He will set priorities, as he does in the very words he speaks to his directee:

> The three attitudinal intentions of helping involve three words: "I instruct you" *(didaskō),* "I urge you" *(parakalō),* and "I love you"

71. Daniel Williams, *The Minister and Care of the Soul* (New York: Harper & Row, 1961), 14.

72. William Oglesby, *Biblical Themes in Pastoral Care* (Nashville: Abingdon, 1980), 18, 25.

> *(agapaō)* . . . [but] there can be no doubt that the primary word is *agapaō*.[73]

What is the spiritual director to do? How is he to "operate" on this "place of the heart"? For an answer we turn to the experience of a notable practitioner of this "art and science," the late Russian emigré priest, Alexander Elchaninov. His initial advice is addressed to the director:

> You cannot cure the soul of others or help people without having changed yourself. You cannot put in order the spiritual economy of others, so long as there is chaos in your own soul. You cannot bring peace to others if you do not have it yourself.[74]

But surely this description applies to the directee's state of heart as well: enslaved to passions of all kinds, spiritually broken, spiritually confused — literally "chaotic." Such a state renders the person incapable of exercising his or her free will, of choosing objectively, because his listening to subjective passions has left him a slave. His emotional life has lost its proper "spiritual economy." Fr. Alexander's advice: "To free ourselves from inner chaos, we must recognize *objective* order."

The heart can also be a place of peace, however, the place where our "spiritual" component is free to show itself clearly. Elchaninov views the healing process as a movement from oneself to communion with God, but this involves a great deal of work done precisely in "the place of the heart":

> The beginning of the spiritual life is to emerge from subjectivity from oneself, to outgrow oneself by entering a communion with the highest principle — with God.[75]

He is *not* advocating here that the healing process be a "gnawing self-analysis" or a "morbid self-flagellation" — an exclusive "concentration on ourselves." Rather he demonstrates a profound understanding of the workings of the heart. A person needs, he says, an

> attentive, calm survey of the soul, a gaze turned inward, a deliberate effort to build up our lives consciously; so that we are not carried

73. *Ibid.*, 29.

74. Fr. Alexander Elchaninov, *The Diary of a Russian Priest,* trans. Helen Iswolsky (Crestwood, NY: St. Vladimir's Seminary Press, 1982, c. 1967), 218.

75. *Ibid.*, 99.

> away by every passing emotion and idea. We are not in the slightest degree our own masters. We need practice, the discipline and attentive determined work upon ourselves.[76]

None of these processes is easy or painless. We tend to use every bit of our "intelligence and imagination" to avoid and to falsify the things we find in our hearts:

> These are like larvae — they stifle the original kernel of personality and multiply, covering it with a parasitic growth. Hence the complexity, entanglements, inevitable falsifications, and loss of personality. . . . Only through strenuous work will the true personality discover itself among all these parasites and find its way through this noisy, motley crowd. One may destroy these parasites by despising or ignoring them and by limiting the sphere of one's interests. But it is almost impossible to achieve this *without the aid of a friend or priest,* for real personality can be so stifled and suppressed that its rediscovery offers the greatest difficulties; the inexperienced prefer the risk of giving new strength to their own larvae. The usual result of this is a muddled life, a wrongly chosen profession; in the worst cases, insanity.[77]

Finally, as Elchaninov himself observes, the connections between spiritual "heart-sickness" and other disorders is complex:

> often . . . a painful condition of the soul, weighted down by sin, entangled and confused by unresolved conflicts, is mistaken for nervous disease.[78]

It is essential that the spiritual director be apprised of both spiritual and psychological expertise if he is to provide effective therapy. We will turn, therefore, to the "direction" component of spiritual direction, and consider methodology.

76. *Ibid.,* 175.
77. *Ibid.,* 64.
78. *Ibid.,* 213.

# 4 The Direction Component: Exploring the Psychological Issues in Spiritual Direction

*An Elder who has mastered spiritual and psychological laws must penetrate the very depths of the human soul . . . in order to diagnose a disease and find a precise method of healing it.*

Ivan Kontzevitch

*Be a companion to those who are sad at heart, with passionate prayer and heartfelt sighs, . . . and support the weak and distressed as far as you are able.*

St. Isaac the Syrian

## Introduction: The Direction Component

For spiritual direction to be reawakened and to thrive as a contemporary ministry, it is not enough to study its theological roots — critical as these may be. We must also investigate issues of *methodology.* This chapter will build upon and complement the previous one, and complete the task of looking at a "direction which is spiritual."

From the outset we must acknowledge that *there is no single method by which to practice spiritual direction.* If history shows that in various ages various elders adopted various approaches and gave various emphases, should we not expect today that each director/directee pair will require a unique strategy? Contemporary literature on spiritual direction confirms that this is indeed so. Since it is impossible to advocate any one method as the "correct" one, I propose to explore a number of methodological issues which are critical in direction, regardless of the specific approach a given practitioner ends up using. Our only absolute criterion is that the theological and spiritual parameters which were set out above not be violated. This is crucial, for these parameters distinguish spiritual direction from other forms of psychological counsel which either necessitate no relationship with or reference to God, or which restrict their attention to one-shot interventions in particular crisis situations.

This exploration of method will not, therefore, rest on any one approach or favor any one "school of thought" in psychology. Nor will it follow an eclectic or syncretistic approach, plucking a "bit of this" and a "bit of that" off the shelves of the various theorists. In many cases this would amount to nothing more than an attempt to baptize a secular anthropological view. Rather, it will seek to uncover those elements of methodology which are both significant in and of themselves, and which are transparent to the theological roots we have just laid bare. When combined with observations of those areas in which the methods of the spiritual director and the psychologist are compatible and/or similar, this should allow us to appreciate the uniqueness of authentic spiritual direction.

If it is, indeed, true that there can be no one method of spiritual direction suitable in every circumstance and for every practitioner, one might legitimately ask, "Why focus on methodology at all?" But it may be, in this case, *more* important to concentrate on method than on theory: the elder, after all, had no interest in placing clinical labels on what he was doing; he did not analyze his ministry — he just performed it. It is the record of his method — his "technique," if we dare use this loaded term — that reveals his "theory," his theological beliefs. Because we have based the previous chapters largely on the literature which these elders left behind, we have already said a good deal about method.

As Perry London has said, concerning other forms of healing:

> The analysis of technique serves understanding more than any other approach to this discipline [psychotherapy], mainly because techniques are relatively concrete things, and . . . also more relevant indices of what actually goes on in any healing therapy.[1]

1. Perry London, *The Modes and Morals of Psychotherapy* (New York: Holt, Rinehart and Winston, 1964), 32.

From this we learn two lessons. First, that the methods of the elders truly indicated what theory — what theological truths — they were "activating." Second, we are reminded that the methodological issues which we will examine forthwith should not be taken lightly. To limit ourselves to theory alone would short-circuit our hope of awakening the *practice* of spiritual direction as a central form of ministry today.

## 1. Methodology: The Uniqueness of Spiritual Direction

There are, as we have seen, obvious points of continuity between certain theories and concepts of general psychological counsel and Christian spiritual direction. There are also numerous lines of discontinuity between them. Looking at both will help us appreciate the uniqueness of the latter. Barry and Connolly alert us to the need "to be aware of the specifically religious resources" of the Christian tradition, which can be "brought to bear to help people live a richer and fuller life." Therefore,

> while we borrow, with gratitude, concepts and practices from the psychological fields, we believe that spiritual direction is a helping relationship distinct from psychotherapy and psychological counseling.

Why? Because spiritual direction

> proposes to help people relate personally to God, to let God relate personally to them, and to enable them to live the consequences of that relationship.[2]

Clearly the methodology used in spiritual direction must reflect this effort. Although the directional/methodological component must include an understanding of what these authors call the "psychological fields," this ministry cannot be reduced to them alone. Sounding very much like Alexander Elchaninov, Barry and Connolly distinguish what is primary from what is subsequent:

> To theological knowledge we must also add, today, some knowledge of modern psychology. Whoever, therefore, wants to help others spir-

2. Barry and Connolly, *Practice*, 136.

> itually must not only be himself a spiritual person . . . but also have sufficient psychological knowledge (without, however, falling into the error of wanting to do psychotherapy and thereby succumbing to the delusion that his psychological knowledge is sufficient for that).[3]

Whatever knowledge can be gained from the "psychological fields" can prove valuable in performing spiritual direction, but must never be looked upon as sufficient in itself. We must allow such information to "speak" to us, yet keep it in its proper place.

What can we expect to reap from these other disciplines? Daniel Williams suggests:

> One of the genuine services of psychology to Christian ministry today has been the recovery of the insight that the element of personal participation in relationship is vital to discovery of both the other person and ourselves.[4]

The methods used in spiritual direction must never be based on any sort of esoteric experience, either on the part of the directee or the director, separate from the other influences and structures in their lives. Rather, all elements of their lives must be brought into the dialogue between them. If one so chooses, spiritual direction *may* be a process of centering, one which views, confronts, interrogates, and guides a person in interpreting the various influences and structures in his or her life. The director must never ignore or circumvent the truth, however, that his directee's perceptions and behavior were not formed in a vacuum. The psychological bases for their formation should be introduced into the dialogue as the directee shares his or her life-story or faith-pilgrimage. Habits, patterns of behavior, ways of thinking and responding, ways of decision-making and choosing, must all be opened up in the process of spiritual direction through self-disclosure — as we have already explored at length. Such self-disclosure will, in turn, produce a spiritual struggle which requires the recognition of how one's life came to be as it is, that is, if one hopes, by God's grace, to make of it what it ought to be. While the *content* may well be shaped out of the various psychological formations of one's past and present, the *struggle* with them for true transformation must clearly be a spiritual one.

3. *Ibid.*, 133.
4. Williams, *Minister and Care*, 21.

Williams further notes that:

> The human being is incredibly complex, and that fact is critically important to the task. . . . This is not to say that we need to have complete scientific knowledge about a person before we can communicate the essential message of salvation. But the spirit of ministry to another human being leads us to respect and use all the knowledge we *do* have.[5]

A brief example is in order. What is called by many the "spirit of love" will not, by itself, necessarily protect a person from the dangerous errors which can lead to spiritual destruction. The director who in this "spirit of love" seeks to direct a paranoid person by "sympathy alone," or an addicted person through "guilt alone," or an abusive husband by "prayer alone," cannot be seen to be truly feeding the hungry person, clothing the naked, healing the sick (see Mt. 25.41-45).[6] Rather, if he fails to apply useful psychological insights to the contortions of mind and behavior which emerge from a directee's past, he might well be inadvertently "enabling" the directee to continue in his or her wrong behavior. Likewise, if he fails to apply the theological principles of growth and struggle to the person's life, he can allow theology itself to be distorted. One can hardly "struggle" unless one knows what to struggle with — or even that one ought to struggle at all.

From our "theological roots" we know that struggle is the methodological *sine qua non* of transformation, and we have suggested that it must be part of an extended *process* rather than being limited to a moment of crisis. Can psychology help us to understand? The "problem" orientation, usually a response to a crisis, can seek to "repair" only one isolated defect at a time; it cannot encompass the full complexity of a person's experience. The layers of influence cannot be peeled off all at once. While some limited benefit can be realized in such situations, a "growth" or "purpose" orientation is more suitable to effecting more global change. When God — and communion with him — are introduced to the equation, this orientation achieves its highest potential.

Can we point to any particular features of how one proceeds in

5. *Ibid.*, 20.

6. The director may realize that referral to a specially trained person is proper, but this does not relieve him of his duty to direct. He must not only "refer" the directee, but continually "confer" with him or her.

"doing" spiritual direction that will set it apart from other forms of helping? No. To attempt this would be as naïve and foolish as to try to establish a uniquely Christian form of surgery — or cooking, or auto mechanics. In any of these disciplines, however, it is not hard to see that there can be a uniquely Christian set of *assumptions, goals,* and *characteristics* which immediately set off their practitioners from non-Christians.

We have already devoted a full chapter to the unique *assumptions* of spiritual direction — the "theological roots" of the ministry. Gary Collins notes, however, that assumptions of this kind are by no means unique to Christianity; no one, in fact, who engages in counseling

> is completely free or neutral in terms of assumptions. We each bring our own viewpoints into the counseling situation and these influence our judgements and comments whether we recognize this or not.[7]

How could one expect the training in and convictions about the attributes of God, the place of the Christian community, the reality of evil and sin in the world, the place of a rule of prayer, etc., not to influence a spiritual director's methodology — whatever that might concretely be?

The general *goals* of spiritual direction can also be expected to influence methodology, and these can almost as certainly be expected to coincide with those of psychological counsel: change bad behaviors, teach self-control, heighten responsibility, and so on. Collins's summary of distinctly Christian (in this case, Western, and Protestant) goals is instructive: "Prayer, reading the scriptures, gentle confrontation with Christian truths, or encouraging persons to become involved in a local Church community, these are common examples."[8] Eastern Christianity adds a whole set of special goals which come out of its moral, ascetical, liturgical, and sacramental experience. One of its most forceful goals is preventing secular goals from predominating! The ultimate goal, of course, is communion with God himself, whose very existence can be ignored or denied in other fields.

The third element of uniqueness is the director's *characteristics.* Here again, there may be points of continuity with other forms of counsel, chiefly because certain elements must be present in a person's makeup for him to function as an effective counselor. C. H. Patterson states that he must be "a real human person" offering "a genuine human relationship to

7. Gary Collins, *Christian Counseling* (Dallas: Word Publishing, 1988), 17.

8. *Ibid.,* 18.

counselees." Often, however, this will be a relationship "characterized not so much by what techniques the therapist uses, as what he is; not so much by what he does, as by the way he does it."[9] One would certainly hope this were true in spiritual direction! But Collins proposes that the spiritual director also be marked by something more — the image of Jesus Christ, the "Wonderful Counselor," and the Holy Spirit, the "Comforter and Paraclete." Through his faith in these two persons of the Holy Trinity, the spiritual director is given the gifts of "love, joy, peace, patience, kindness, generosity, faithfulness, gentleness, and self-control" (Gal. 5.22) through the action of the Holy Spirit who teaches all things that Christ himself said (Jn. 14.16, 26; 16.7-15). These "additional" characteristics — which have always been regarded as essential qualities in the elder in the Eastern Christian tradition — are certainly critical today to *any* Christian seeking to practice spiritual direction.

Thus we see points of continuity and discontinuity between spiritual direction and other forms of counsel. Continuity where one would expect it — in those areas where being simply human is enough (in the popular understanding, this time); and discontinuity where God must be the source, goal, and focus.

## 2. Patterns in Methodology

Certain set patterns, which one might also call "processes," ought to be present in the *praxis* of spiritual direction, and these unfold in a somewhat sequential manner, as phases or stages. For instance, any method which one might consider adopting should at an early stage incorporate some means of guaranteeing *objectification* and *interpretation.* If Dyckman and Carroll are correct in their assessment that "a spiritual director is often, but never exclusively, a counselor,"[10] then perhaps analyzing how these patterns are used in practice will help us differentiate between counseling per se and spiritual direction.

How does the spiritual director seek to objectify reality? First

9. C. H. Patterson, *Theories of Counseling and Psychotherapy* (New York: Harper & Row, 1973), 535.

10. Katherine Marie Dyckman and L. Patrick Carroll, *Inviting the Mystic, Supporting the Prophet* (New York: Paulist Press, 1981), 22.

and foremost, as we have indicated, by listening. "Nothing a director does is more important than to be a listening ear for another."[11] This quality cuts across every — and any — method of direction. There is nothing strange in this. Why, after all, would a person choose to speak to another about the intimate dimensions of his or her life unless something deeply human called out for objectification? For getting out whatever is inside that *needs* to get out.

> We need to speak to another in order to put our deepest fears, hopes, and dreams out in front of ourselves where we can look at them. The very process of articulation can itself be a healing experience.[12]

For the elder accompanying a person on his or her faith-pilgrimage, listening was at least as important a methodological concern as was speaking. Getting things "out," in the process of a trusting self-disclosure, is the best way of discovering what is going on in the struggle to grow toward communion with God and one's fellows. Because the elder's short-term goal was to objectify the directee's experience, he set no fixed bounds for the dialogue. The whole person and all of life served as its raw materials. Anything significant to the person's struggle was significant to the director's listening ear — even when the director might have preferred, perhaps for the time being, not to have dealt with something the directee wished to bring out.

Objectification, then, begins with very attentive listening, but can not end there:

> The unspoken word, the tone of voice . . . help constitute the data of objectification. . . . Sometimes the use of a journal . . . may help to externalize the deepest feeling and become an apt subject matter for direction. . . . We do whatever we can to creatively help another *see.* At this stage the listening director speaks little, asks supportive questions, clarifies what is obscure, and allows silence so that what has been spoken may sink in.[13]

The level of the director's activity depends on what is necessary to help the "objective facts" emerge. Common techniques in objectification in-

11. *Ibid.,* 22.
12. *Ibid.,* 23.
13. *Ibid.*

clude *confirming, confronting,* and *teaching.* He listens in order to *confirm* anything that is God-like, alive, and growing in the directee. "Most people have very poor self-images," Dyckman and Carroll write, "and find their stories discouraging and depressing, or worse, boring. The sensitive listener hears the bright spots and underlines them."[14]

He also will know when to *confront.* Confrontation does not mean that one has stopped listening; rather, that as an active and compassionate listener, he shifts gears in order gently to unmask illusions, point out inconsistencies, or recall to the directee's memory aspirations or admissions made earlier.

Finally, objectification may include elements of *teaching.* Sometimes right at the outset there are things that need to be taught, facts that need to be set straight, responses to realities which cannot wait to be corrected.

Many forms of counseling and therapy are content when they have completed the objectification pattern. In spiritual direction, it must indeed form the first stage in any method, but it cannot, in and of itself, bring about healing. A second stage must follow, which is termed by Dyckman and Carroll as *interpretation.* Here we begin to focus more intently on the uniqueness of spiritual direction. Its practitioner's role

> differs significantly from the role of psychiatric counselor or psychologist. The spiritual director specifically desires to help people see their experience in light of faith, to see the journey as a *faith* journey, to envision and trust God's guiding hand in the process.[15]

This means that both the director and the directee are to take the raw material, newly objectified, and interpret its meaning in terms of God's calling, challenging, leading, etc. This material constitutes a type of "life-hermeneutic."

However, in order to fulfill such a pattern of interpretation, the raw material must be measured against something. That "something" is the Gospel, by which "we do not mean primarily the written word, but rather him about whom the word is written and who is, in fact, the Word."[16] The "image of God" anthropology of the Eastern Church demanded that both elder and directee agree to accept this pattern.

14. *Ibid.*, 24.
15. *Ibid.*
16. *Ibid.*, 25.

When this happens in a contemporary scenario, the director will have permission, as it were, to "appropriate" the person's life-story around the life-story of Jesus Christ, with natural allowances for the different context. This is even true when a specific crisis event crops up in the process of direction. Indeed, in the midst of any crisis — death, grief, sickness, divorce, etc. — there resides a call to grow, a call to "stretch," giving the opportunity to interpret the event according to the death/resurrection motif, whose highest expression is the Crucified and Risen One himself. The "compost heap" is churned up to produce new life from life's cast-offs.

The interpretation pattern allows the director to see the long-range rhythms and patterns of life in which the directee's decisions have led him or her — and will continue to lead him or her — either toward or away from God. The realization that the dialogue is really a *trialogue* — the third Person being God — causes the director to be

> constantly aware that the real director is the Holy Spirit, and that the interpretation of the experiences may more properly and ultimately come from God out of prayer, rather than simply in dialogue between two parties.[17]

Of course, this relieves the director of none of his investment in the process. While attempting to be transparent to God's Holy Spirit, he will have to persist in the dialogue with his directee until *something* happens: clarity is achieved, an acceptable pattern of perception and behavior emerges, or an appropriate corrective action presents itself. This may require several sessions, and should incorporate such elements as invitation to prayer, reading of pertinent passages of scripture, reading other helpful materials, writing — whatever it is that will help further interpret the person's life-story, his faith-pilgrimage.

A real distinction can thus be drawn between spiritual direction and secular counsel, precisely in the application of this pattern of interpretation. Anyone who seeks to help another must be aware of the subjective presuppositions which he or she brings to the healing dialogue, but since both spiritual director and directee *agree* beforehand on the theological roots — rather, the primacy of the Good News about Jesus Christ — they will interpret the raw materials presented in a radi-

17. *Ibid.*, 26.

cally different way from those outside the Church. Dyckman and Carroll summarize:

> As a director we are not just enabling people to reflect upon and integrate life, as a good counselor would do, but to do so in the light of who they are called to become in fidelity to the Gospel. This . . . is the distinct and decided difference between counseling and spiritual direction.[18]

Is there anything that guarantees that these two methodological patterns, objectification and interpretation, will bear the fruit of healing and growth? We touched upon it at the start of this section, and now will develop it more fully: the function of listening.

### 3. Listening: More than Hearing

The *praxis* of spiritual direction will always require that the director do more *listening* than hearing. When someone asks a question it can either be "listened to" or "heard." In colloquial speech the two functions are most often used interchangeably, but in the practice of ministry they must be distinguished. There is an important *functional* difference between how one uses one's faculties in the two cases. In truly listening, the ear absorbs the messages of the directee's disclosure at a far deeper level than does the ear that is content merely to hear. One can call this type of attentiveness "*active* listening."

> Research has verified the beneficial effects of listening and has helped to define the type of listening that is most therapeutic. *Active* listening is a primary element of any truly therapeutic intervention.[19]

The *hearing* ear may certainly recognize that a question has been asked in such a way as to form a response, enter a discussion, etc., but it will not attain the *depth* of the listening ear. When listening is attentive and empathetic, "it is the one intervention which is not merely 'necessary,' but entirely sufficient for fostering healing and growth."[20] Because the spiritual

18. *Ibid.*, 27.

19. J. Moursand, *The Process of Counseling and Therapy* (Englewood Cliffs, NJ: Prentice-Hall, 1985), 3.

20. G. Thompson, "Listening is More than Hearing," *Ministry* (Sept. 1987), 11-13.

director is a person invited into another's life-story as his or her "companion," he is obliged to use his listening ear; this is the initial requirement of becoming a "soul-friend," a "spiritual physician," a "trusted other":

> whatever we do in a healing therapy is accomplished by means of true communication. That is what we do with others. Such communication is *listening*, . . . listening and then responding.[21]

Entering another person's soul is so delicate a matter that we need to know what constitutes *active* listening in order to avoid falling into "involuntary hearing." Four characteristics of active listening can be distinguished[22] within our objectification/interpretation stages:

a. It is *intentional.* When invited to do so by the directee, the director will endeavor to enter the experience of his or her life-story as fully and as accurately as possible. This is particularly crucial in the early stages of objectification.

b. It is *focused.* While the directee may refer to many things and many persons external to him- or herself, the director will concentrate on what the directee is disclosing about his or her inner self. This means that, although these other things and persons are important and make up some of the raw material of the dialogue, the director must focus on the directee: what a given experience *means to him* in his concrete living situation, his attitudes, perceptions, behavior — the moral and spiritual issues of his interior being. This too properly belongs to the stage of objectification.

c. It is *interpretive.* The director must also listen to what the directee is *not* saying. The second stage of the methodology — Interpretation — begins here. In order to understand how the directee feels about an experience, one must take into account *how* he or she is relating the events. In gently prodding to uncover what is meant, the director must be careful to factor in his own subjectivity, and consider his initial interpretation strictly tentative. Only by measuring the person's perceptions and behavior against the Image of God anthropology or the Gospel can a more objective interpretation be reached. Of course, should a blatantly evil action be revealed, something obviously antithetical to the Gospel and the directee's spiritual growth, the director may well discern that an immediate response is called for, and formulate a "working"

21. Moursand, *Process,* 14.

22. Thompson, "Listening," 11. I am endebted to Thompson for the terminology, although I have adapted it somewhat to my own purpose.

interpretation by which the directee will begin to see such negative behavior in an ongoing pattern.

d. It is *articulated.* Unless the director conveys properly and sensitively that he has truly listened to his directee, any advice he may give will obviously receive a limited reception. He can communicate that he is actively listening through regular "perception checks" in the course of the dialogue, through either *interpretive questions* or *declarative statements* aimed at bringing to bear the theological implications of the experience that is being revealed. We have seen this technique used by the ancient elders, for whom humility was a central ritual and who consciously resisted presumption of divine omniscience.

Besides these four characteristics of active listening, there are additional methodological issues related to the subject which both are consistent with the theological roots of spiritual direction and function within the objectification/interpretation pattern. These are *person-listening, dialogue,* and *reporting.*

A spiritual director must be more a *person*-listener than a topic-listener. This does not mean that the topics introduced to the dialogue by the directee are unimportant, but rather that the director must focus his primary attention on the larger picture of the person as a whole, in his or her living relationship with God and neighbor. He will listen actively to the topic at hand, but within this broader context. Because growth and healing occur only when a person is pushed beyond any topic he or she may be presenting, no single communication — no matter how significant — can be considered in ultimate terms. Every topic should be viewed as a gateway or avenue into the person's total interior life.

> Close, analytical, even critical listening to topic content is not to be put down. It is essential to living. But it is listening to understand the *person* that best qualifies as "active." For the truly listening ear, it is not so important to understand that which is upsetting to another, as to understand his experience of *being* upset . . . what it means to his functioning.[23]

Listening to the total person presupposes *dialogue* between director and directee. The trusted companion on the faith-pilgrimage must resist the temptation to resort to monologue. This does not mean, of course, that he will not direct and confront the directee. Rather this

23. *Ibid.*, 12.

means that *how* he does this will remain consistent with the spiritual nature of his task. Paul Tournier observes that most people interact with others primarily through the presentation of false *personae* (what he terms "personages") — so that communication between them amounts to little more than "dialogues of the deaf." Indeed, the quality of active listening distinguishes between an "individual" and a true person: "an individual 'associates,' while a person 'communicates.'"[24] In any conversation the forms used may make it appear that communication is taking place, but very often it is not, since the hearer — as distinct from "listener" — is not attuned to the speaker; both are preoccupied with presenting the correct *persona* to each other. The spiritual director must do whatever is necessary to create true dialogue if he hopes to engage his directee's interior experience.

"Dialogue at its best connotes two or more [*sic*] people interacting on a common level, each listening intently to, and trying to understand, the other."[25] Without this kind of listening, a proper response is impossible. For example, when the spiritual director finds his "trusting other" in the dialogue speaking in the third person about someone or something "out there," he will realize that the dialogue has diminished and must force it back on track — back to a close focus on the directee's own person. Were he only "hearing" the content of the disclosure, no correction would be possible. He cannot allow the disclosure to become an intellectual monologue on which he will, from time to time, pass comment. He would then be a lecturer rather than an actively listening companion.

Active listening also requires proper *questioning*. Historically, various lists of questions were prepared to aid the spiritual director in his ministry. In the context of methodology, we might well ask, "How does the person being questioned perceive the experience?"

> Questions have their place. Anyone who has seen a skillful lawyer break down a carefully constructed lie knows the value of effective question[s] . . . *as weapons*. The trouble is that that is precisely the way questions are commonly experienced — as *weapons of attack*.[26]

24. Paul Tournier, *The Meaning of Persons* (New York: Harper, 1957), 27. The problem of one's "*persona*" serving as an impediment to true dialogue between persons is the theme of this excellent study.

25. Thompson, "Listening," 12.

26. *Ibid.*, 26; Thompson is citing Jacques Lalanne.

This reaction is entirely natural. From childhood most of the questions put to us are really veiled accusations: "Where were you?" "Why are you late?" The spiritual director must ask questions, to be sure, but he must take care that they not be perceived in this way, or surely the directee will distance him- or herself and transmit as little information as possible. The director will most often find himself or herself obliged to ask questions after picking up signs of *anxiety* in the directee — a softer-than-usual voice, phrases about things hoped and prayed for but not received, and so on. These indicate that he or she is particularly vulnerable and needful of reassurance that the director is truly a companion in the faith-pilgrimage. The director, in turn, cannot afford to hide behind his questions and yet hope for trusting disclosure to happen. He cannot use questions to control the directee — that is what accusations do. Rather, his questions must be immediately understandable as an attempt to uncover the truth in order to introduce the light of healing and growth. His questioning must encourage *reporting.*

> Reporting and questioning may seem similar on the surface, but there is one key difference: reporting includes a description of the reporter's interior experience, rather than a mere question of his "feelings." . . . [Reporting] is an affirmation, a statement, a disclosing of myself. "What did you mean by that!" can become "Can you explain what you mean?" . . . [Such reporting] tends to diffuse any sense of attack that might be perceived in a question.[27]

The director will know whether a question was successful if he is able to use the response to "report back" to the directee what he heard (or rather, "actively listened to"). This technique can help create a non-attacking, non-accusing atmosphere. The process is initiated by truly active listening, creating within the director an empathy for his directee's experience. If the director remains in touch with this empathy within his own heart, he will communicate to the directee a sense of paternity — without avoiding the truth — which engenders life-giving and healing-promoting trust. This feedback will encourage trusting self-disclosure rather than withdrawal from veiled accusations. Because spiritual direction is a process, it is critical that nothing be

27. *Ibid.*, 13.

allowed to cause it to break down. The directee simply must know that he or she is being listened to. This will embue in his or her soul the joy which the Psalmist felt:

> I love the Lord because he has listened to my voice and my supplications. Because he has inclined his ear to me, therefore I will call upon him. (Ps. 116.1-2)

The actively listening ear of the director will help the directee know that he may also "call upon *him*" as together they move toward healing and growth in the *inner way.*

## 4. The Meeting in the Method: Director and Directee

What happens when director and directee meet? How is the meeting to be understood methodologically? A number of modern theorists have made valuable contributions in this area, including C. J. Steckel and Thomas Oden. A third colleague, Theron Nease, provides a useful introduction to the question:

> Persons seeking care, understanding, and acceptance of the Shepherd, are not just seeking relief from these needs and distress. They are also declaring that they have lost their "counsel" and the "right ordering" of life. Instead of answers, they are seeking to regain their counsel, and they want to seek out the values, meaning, and purpose which will assist them.[28]

The spiritual director who hopes to assist such persons in their quest must be acutely aware of those issues which their life circumstances impose on them. These surely will color the dialogue between director and directee. Indeed, in each pattern of objectification and interpretation such issues will arise.

Steckel focuses on the *directee,* and raises five issues sure to be of importance to him or her in dialogue with the director:

28. T. S. Nease, "Pastoral Care: Generativity or Stagnation?" *Pastoral Psychology* 26.4 (1978), 229-39.

a. The directee's *central assumptions*, "those few fundamental, largely unconscious approaches we take to life." These generally develop early in life and become integral parts of our character. Typical statements of these assumptions are "The world is a friendly place" or "The world is an unfriendly place"; "I am a good person" or "I am a bad person."[29]

b. The directee's *core convictions*, those "basic beliefs of which we are aware, and which we state as truths of our lives." These are related to and *arise* from our central assumptions. In turn, every assumption leads to a conviction. Convictions can be seen as

> explicit statements arising out of the central assumptions (in which case there is *congruence* between life and belief); or as ideals which we hold for ourselves (and others) at precisely those points where central assumptions seem negative (in which case there is *incongruity*).[30]

An example of congruence of conviction and assumption would be, "I believe in love [core conviction] and I am loved [central assumption]." Incongruity would show up in a statement like, "I believe in love [core conviction], but I am *un*lovable [central assumption]." Central assumptions deal with self-perceptions; core convictions deal with faith. Faith issues, after all, always manifest themselves as a synthesis of assumption and conviction, and these can either be congruous or incongruous one to the other. Determining which is the case for any given directee is a major responsibility of the director.

c. The directee's need for *cultural analysis*, "the way in which we become self-conscious of the images and values from culture which have religious significance."[31] The Apostle Paul warned, "Do not be conformed to this world" (Rom. 12.2), and the spiritual director must adopt a methodology that provides for affirming those cultural values which promote theological truths and rejecting those which run contrary to the truth.

d. The directee's need for the *tradition of the faith community*, the way our

> faith tradition has shaped our perceptions of reality, our ways of knowing and believing, the relationship of society which our tradi-

29. C. J. Steckel, "A Model for Theological Interpretation in Pastoral Care," *Pastoral Psychology* 26.4 (1978), 253-62.

30. *Ibid.*

31. *Ibid.*, 232.

> tions exemplify, and the ways in which faith identity gets built into personal identity.[32]

This should be a particularly crucial concern for Eastern Christians living in North America, where much of the tradition is alien to the majority faiths and stands at odds with the tenets of American civil religion. The director should be expected to have a fairly strong grounding in this area by reason of his formal theological training.

e. The directee's need for the *scholarly disciplines.* Again, the modern milieu makes this a particularly acute problem. The media constantly bombard people with aberrant views on faith and ethics, raising the most diverse questions in directees' minds. They should feel confident in bringing these — both "the routine as well as the novel demands" — to the director, along with the context in which the question arose, and come away with "a sense of clear understanding . . . of the options available."[33]

If Steckel focuses more on the directee, Thomas Oden's attention, by contrast, is turned on the *director* and his need to integrate the explicit theological beliefs which he holds, with the implicit method of spiritual direction which he practices. His goal must be "to clarify the analogy between God's mode of being in the world, and the [director's] mode of being with the . . . person."[34] Oden's, too, is a five-part inquiry.

a. The director's method must show *empathy,* allowing him to place himself "in the frame of reference of another, perceiving the world as he or she [the directee] perceives it, and sharing his world with him."[35] The author bases this requirement on the Incarnation:

> God assumes in Jesus Christ our frame of reference, entering into our human situation of finitude and estrangement, sharing our human condition even unto death.[36]

Oden warns, however, that this is only an analogy. The director's ability to enter his directee's frame of reference will always be limited by his own human "historical perspective, cultural prejudices, and distor-

32. *Ibid.*
33. *Ibid.*, 233.
34. Oden, *Kerygma and Counseling,* 48.
35. *Ibid.*, 50.
36. *Ibid.*

tions."[37] An expression of empathy, it is hoped, will free the directee sufficiently to allow him or her to gain increased self-knowledge.

b. The director's method must show *congruence* — inner consistency, the fact that he is in touch with his own inner life, through prayer and the experience of struggle — in order to build in the directee the confidence needed to disclose anything and everything without fear that the director's integrity will weaken or be shattered. The author again finds an analogy in God's own "method":

> God participates in the human estrangement without being estranged from himself, much as the [director] participates in the other's estrangement without losing his self-identity.[38]

c. The director's method must show *acceptance;* it must be "nonjudgmental." At first glance this would appear to be antithetical, especially to Eastern Christian theology, since judgments have to be made. We have already differentiated between acceptance and approval — when we judge, we judge a person's behavior, not his or her being. In this light Oden's point is both valid and significant. When a directee knows that he or she has been personally accepted by the director, he is more likely to disclose his various predicaments and experiences, and thereby to come to grips with them, and thus be healed. The author has another ready analogy:

> God accepts us radically. It does not mean that our phoney human existence is somehow magically changed into utopia. But it does mean that we are accepted *amid* our phoniness.[39]

d. The director's method must include *permissiveness.* By this he does *not* mean that the directee should be given *carte blanche* to do anything he or she wants in life. Rather, it refers to the atmosphere of freedom and trust that should pervade the director/directee relationship. The directee should be "permitted" to be him- or herself, to discover through the patterns of objectification and interpretation the person that he or she truly is. This is a prerequisite for any change or transformative growth to occur.

37. *Ibid.*, 55.
38. *Ibid.*, 57.
39. *Ibid.*, 62.

e. The director's method must be formed by *unconditional positive regard.* Of Oden's five dimensions, this one brings us closest to the method of the elder. The director must manifest "a caring that is not possessive, and which demands no personal gratification." The author expounds:

> It is an atmosphere which simply demonstrates "I care"; not "I care for you *if* you behave thus and so." How does the kerygma's witness to the *agapē* of God illuminate [this]? . . . Even as God unconditionally loves the sinner in order to free him from the self-righteousness, anxiety, guilt, and defensiveness that prevent him from loving his neighbor. . . . So does the [directee] experience in some sense what appears to be a relationship of unconditional positive regard which frees him to value others anew in light of his new self-valuation.[40]

## 5. Responsibility and Confrontation: Contemporary Models Which Conflict

In the contemporary practice of this ministry, special attention must be given to two issues: *responsibility* and *confrontation.* Allowing for them in one's specific methodology will further clarify the differences between spiritual direction and psychological counsel. We have mentioned both issues before, but the question remains, "How are they to be *practiced?*" "How are they vital to healing and growth?"

Both issues figure prominently in secular counseling's efforts to foster healing and growth. Furthermore, the particular interpretations given to them in such secular systems have spilled over into a variety of *popular* notions which directly or indirectly influence the way in which we all understand these matters today. Many of these prominent systems stand in direct conflict with the way in which Eastern Christian theology and spiritual direction have historically treated these subjects. These points of conflict will be our major focus in the pages ahead.

We will examine three leading orientations or models, not in order to explore them thoroughly — each would warrant a major study of its

40. *Ibid.,* 73-74.

own. Rather, we will look for those features within each model that make it impossible for spiritual direction to utilize it as the uniquely "correct" model for its own task, even if spiritual directors can find some elements in them that can help in their ministry. The three models selected are the *nondirective, behavior modification,* and *psychoanalysis.*

I could also have included various *developmental* schemes, such as those put forth by Fowler, Kohlberg, Erickson, and others. These are well-represented in contemporary literature and have much to say to our methodological concerns, since the spiritual director must certainly be sensitive to "where a person is" in terms of age and development. The notion of not differentiating in the kind of direction given to a twenty-five-year-old as to a fifty-five-year-old, harkens back to the Syriac father's remarks about a mother feeding her widely spaced children identical meals (see p. 38). Certainly any spiritual director will want to become familiar with the major concerns, orientations, and issues activated at various "stages" in the human life cycle, but the developmentalists propose nothing which differs radically enough from the other theorists to warrant considering them at length.

Each of these orientations — each model of thought and behavior — utilizes a therapy that can easily distort Christian morality. As we have already seen, methodology and practices clearly reveal what is central to theory and belief in any discipline. "What is considered operative (regardless of rhetoric or theoretical trappings) will find its way into the basic everyday methodology of the practitioner."[41]

A critical point to understand as we explore our three chosen secular theories is that often these orientations replace a "moral" model with a "medical" one, and the results are most often devastating from the standpoint of our theology. This, of course, has nothing to do with medical language per se; the fathers and elders of the Church frequently employed such terminology. Nor does it deny the persuasive experimental evidence that chemical malfunctions can indeed cause distortions in perception[42]

41. Jay E. Adams, *Pastoral Counseling* (Grand Rapids: Baker Book House, 1975), 1.

42. See Abram Hoffer and Humphry Osmond, *How to Live with Schizophrenia* (New York: University Books, 1966). The authors proposed that organic causes can easily distort one's perceptive system. Their thesis is that when adrenachrome is formed in the body, it breaks down into other chemicals. However, in some individuals this either does not occur rapidly enough or breaks down into abnormal chemicals; in either case the result is a distortion of reality. Although the evidence for such somatic theories is

and, doubtless, other organic and somatic factors do contribute to the tribulations and abnormalities of humanity. Rather, it is a purely methodological consideration, based on the observed tendency of these models to neglect and negate responsibility and confrontation.

That is, the "medical model" all too easily bypasses the responsibility of the directee freely to *change* his or her behavior, and leads to the diminishment of the human person — the αὐτεξούσιον [*autexousion:* the "one granted free-will"] in the image of God. It views the directee always as a victim, always passive; never a violator, never an active participant. This extreme position can be termed *allogenic,*[43] because it always looks for an external cause (ἄλλος [*allos:* "other"]) rather than accepting one's own responsibility (αὐτός [*autos:* "self"]). We will encounter these two terms throughout our discussion of the three psychological models.

It is true that people *are* sometimes victims. Things do happen to them, leaving a mark, causing great harm to their perceptions and behavior.[44] Every human being has the potential for carrying within him- or herself a "wounded child" — one who is in need of healing. But a radical emphasis on the medical model *always* relegates sin to sickness, always views the person as an "irresponsible pawn," moved at the mercy of something external being *done* to him or her. In moral terms, these people are always "victims" of their conscience, never violators of it. O. H. Mowrer attacks both the Freudian ethic and evangelical religion for acquiescing to this model (the latter he also accuses of "selling out its birthright"). He claims that for several decades we looked upon the whole matter of sin

---

not conclusive, we should certainly leave room for the possibility that organic causes can underlie some mental and emotional problems. In a sense, organically based problems are not the responsibility of the person; however, this does not invalidate the contention that in terms of spiritual direction the "moral model," with its requirement that responsibility is the only true route to healing and growth, is superior to the "medical model," which looks entirely to organic causes of disorders.

43. See Thomas Szasz, *Psychiatry and Responsibility* (Princeton, NJ: Van Nostrand, 1962). The author claims that the *allogenic* view leads to a general degradation of human responsibility. Even the mentally ill, he claims, should be held responsible for what they do, rather than being mechanically manipulated as though they were irresponsible pawns.

44. See John and Paul Sanford's two studies: *Healing the Wounded Spirit* (Tulsa, OK: Victory House, 1985) and *The Transformation of the Inner Man* (Tulsa, OK: Victory House, 1982). Both provide excellent analyses of the "wounded child" which each of us can carry within ourselves.

and moral accountability as a great incubus and acclaimed our liberation from it as epoch-making. But at length we have discovered that to be "free" in this sense, that is, to have the excuse of being "sick" rather than sinful, is to court the danger of also becoming lost.[45]

While acknowledging that people may indeed be "victimized" by their circumstances, we must not perpetuate a cult of victimhood. For example, there are times when a person truly needs to seek psychiatric help. And if the patient is also a spiritual directee, he or she must never be allowed to evade a proper sense of responsibility to get such help. A responsible reaction to a given predicament — one which exercises God-given free will correctly — always carries virtue within it. A person might indeed be a victim of his or her past — culture, parents, etc. — but he need not remain trapped in it, chained to it, as he will be in an exclusively allogenic orientation. The medical model must leave space for a "moral model," one which considers the impact of the allogenic features in one's life-story but refuses to succumb to medical reasoning as an exclusive method.

a. The first orientation which often conflicts methodologically with spiritual direction is the *Rogerian* model. The American psychologist Carl Rogers (born 1931) advocates a "reflective" type of counseling, using a "client-oriented" and "nondirective" approach.[46] The weaknesses of this approach include a failure clearly to delineate between acceptance and approval — an absolute necessity in spiritual direction. Although one can find isolated elements in the Rogerian model which might coincide with the approach I have advocated in practicing spiritual direction, it must be viewed as radically unorthodox as a whole. It proposes that a person direct his or her own interview, weight the issues him- or herself, gain whatever insights he or she can, and make decisions based entirely on his or her own resources. No objective "reference point" is invoked, and there is therefore no possibility for objectification. Indeed, Rogerian counseling does not "direct" at all. It presents no basis for responsibility and risks no confrontation in any shape. Any advice, opinions, reflection — or, indeed, "direction" — is strictly taboo. The

45. O. Hobart Mowrer, "Sin, the Lesser of Two Evils," *American Psychologist* 15 (1960), 301-4; see also his *The Crisis in Psychiatry and Religion* (Princeton, NJ: Van Nostrand, 1961), 60.

46. See Carl Rogers's introduction to Charles Curran's *Personality Factors in Counseling* (New York: Grune and Stratton, 1945).

counselor's task is merely to hold up a "mirror" before the client, since Rogers holds that the human being needs nothing outside him- or herself; he or she is the source of everything necessary for the solution of any problem:

> He makes every move in accordance with one fundamental conviction — that the person is capable, once he has been set free from tensions and has achieved clearer insight, of formulating and carrying through a sound solution of his life's difficulties.[47]

Such "nondirective" counsel is widespread among Christian practitioners today. Rogers is greatly admired by them for holding that "the nondirective viewpoint places high value on every individual to be psychologically independent."[48]

The conflict between Rogerianism and spiritual direction lies not only in its radical emphasis on individual autonomy apart from God; not only in its failure to deal with the reality of sin and repentance; not only in its lack of an objective source outside the person's own opinions (a function we see properly residing in the Gospel and the image of God theology) — but at the deepest level of *methodology* itself. How could a "nondirective" approach fail to be at odds with spiritual *direction?* It refuses to remind the person of his or her responsibility. It will not confront one with one's actions. It contents itself with "mirroring" one's current state, and depends for a resolution on one's own innate abilities while in this state. Such an approach cannot promote the healing and growth which Christianity demands.

Can anything be salvaged from this orientation? Can the spiritual director use the "mirror" in his ministry? Yes, he must help his directees see themselves as they truly are. But the scriptures themselves warn about the limitations of the mirror; it allows us to know only in part (1 Cor. 13.12), and our recollection is so short that we soon forget the manner of person that we beheld in its reflection (Jas. 1.23). Ultimately, where a model makes no provision for responsibility and confrontation — where the grounds for morality do not exist — that model must be said to fail for spiritual direction. Rogerianism is no better than the exclusive "medical model," for it falls prey to the same limitations.

47. *Ibid*, xix.

48. Carl Rogers, *Counseling and Psychotherapy* (Boston: Houghton Mifflin, 1942), 127.

b. The second orientation we will examine is the *behavioral* model. Also known by the terms "behaviorism" or "behavior modification," its prime proponent and theoretician was B. F. Skinner (1904-1990). At first glance, it would appear that there should be much overlap between this model and spiritual direction and that borrowable elements should abound, since both are concerned with changing behavior. In fact, this is not the case. The behavioral model takes a radically allogenic view of moral responsibility: human behavior is subject to manipulation and control by the external environment. The human being is, thereby, dehumanized. Writes Adams:

> The methodology makes all plain: Utopia is scientifically possible because science has shown that *man is only another animal.* That is the fundamental Skinnerian presupposition. More complex than other animals, more difficult to control . . . but more than an animal? — no. Since he is not, he can be trained and controlled as every other animal may be: by the manipulation of the environment.[49]

Such an orientation, of course, forces Skinnerians to be avowedly "anti-religious" (which is not required in Rogerianism). Furthermore, their models exclude the existence of values; "values are not empirically observable. All there is to man is behavior, and the sooner we learn this, the better." Responsibility is swept aside by a rigid determinism and operant conditioning. In fact, Skinner not only denigrates responsibility, "but denies that which gives dignity to man: the image of God in which he is created."[50]

The methodological conflict with spiritual direction is obvious. This model allows no room for the essential undergirding of the "spiritual component." Freedom, sin, guilt, repentance, etc., find no place here. The person is manipulated rather than converted; reinforced rather than persuaded. Even though the human being shares certain characteristics with the animals created by God, spiritual direction supposes that he enjoys a special dignity because of the "image" which forms a constituent element in his nature. It is this element which imposes a moral relationship on the person relative to God and neighbor.

The behaviorist method conflicts with the moral demands of spiritual direction; after all, the robot can bear no responsibility. Where it

49. Adams, *Pastoral Counseling,* 7.
50. *Ibid.*

allows confrontation at all, it is only to force the person to conform to the predominant control of the environment, which the behaviorist believes to be the panacea for all the world's troubles. Like the Rogerian model, behaviorism diminishes the human person and, by removing his dignity, undermines all that has been assumed by the theological roots of the inner way. It is insufficient as a method for practicing spiritual direction.

c. The third orientation, and the one closest to the "medical" model, is the *Freudian*. In order to understand its presuppositions, we must look at its author's attacks on religion in general, and Christianity in particular.[51] Sigmund Freud (1856-1939) taught that religions are illusions, born of the great and untamed fears of the universe that surrounded primitive humankind. Religious longings are a sign of human neuroses: every human is born with driving instincts which he desires to express, but since the full expression of these would conflict with the wishes of other individuals in society — as well as with the proper development of civilization in general — certain "codes of conduct" have had to be invented in order to avoid anarchy.

Thus for Freud, morality is no more than the result of societal norms. Primitive humankind enforced such norms through the invention of "gods" which controlled their actions, sanctioned the code, and kept them in a state of perpetual infancy. When humans "grow up" they no longer need religion.[52] What remains is the internal guarantor and enforcer of the moral code — and, thereby, the preserver of society: the "superego," a *partial* analogy to the Christian conscience. Its operation

51. See especially Freud's *Civilization and Its Discontents* (New York: W. W. Norton, 1961); *The Future of an Illusion* (Garden City, NY: Doubleday, 1961); and *Totem and Taboo* (New York: Random House, 1946). I recommend studying these, despite the fact that Freud wrote thousands of pages, changed his positions and theories often, and sometimes contradicted himself. Furthermore, it should be understood that many psychiatrists and psychoanalysts have distanced themselves from Freud's presuppositions even while continuing to utilize his methodology in seeking to uncover those truths of an individual's motivation with which he or she may be unwilling to come to terms — or about which he or she may be totally unaware. This is an admirable task, and it shares a common concern with spiritual direction. The difference, however, is that spiritual direction will always seek a deeper communion with God — something which may not necessarily be a specific goal of the psychoanalyst.

52. See Heinrich Meng and Ernst Freud (eds.), *Psychoanalysis and Faith* (New York: Basic Books, 1963); and Wayne Oates, *What Religion Says about Psychology* (New York: Association Press, 1958).

is not prompted by God, and in terms of pure function, it lacks many of the characteristics of the conscience as historically defined; since it is intended solely to prevent violations of the code, it is strictly punitive and negative.

The method which emerged from Freud's theories is called *psychoanalysis.* At the most fundamental level, it consists of traveling back into a person's past in order to unearth the forces, events, personalities, etc., which have influenced him or her. The person's dreams, slips of the tongue, etc., all point to deep-seated influences which have been impressed upon his or her overly-strict superego. When the latter comes into violent collision with the person's instinct (labelled the "id"), the resulting conflict can become lodged in the unconscious realms, resulting in crippling guilt, neuroses, and even psychoses. Psychoanalysis seeks to enter into and investigate these operations of the person's subsconscious life, and to reduce the conflict between the rigid and punishing superego and the desirous id. This is done often by diffusing the power of the superego.

The conflict between Freud's presuppositions — even among those of his disciples who have denounced the anti-religious tone of his teachings — and those of historical Christianity should be abundantly obvious, but the tension between psychoanalysis and spiritual direction is not limited to theory. Nor is it limited to the methodology which the two employ when dealing with disease, excessive guilt, rigidity, neurosis, psychosis, etc. Of course, it is true that many forms of psychiatry — and the prescription of medications — are legitimately helpful in bringing relief to sufferers. Furthermore the psychiatrist's search for truth is itself admirable[53] — even if the truth sought after is narrowly restricted to the motivations behind the patient's behavior. The true conflict can arise when this model is applied exclusively and allowed to relieve the person of his or her responsibility before God, which spiritual direction sees as the basis for responsibility toward one's neighbor. The entire spiritual dimension — from fidelity to the Gospel of Jesus Christ through the "image of God" theology, down to such practical elements as maintaining a rule of prayer — demands that a person take responsibility for what he or she is and does. There are "givens" against which a person is measured and which lead to healing and growth. Even when psychoanalysis makes room for God — and today it sometimes does — com-

53. See the observations by Lila Kalinich in "Psychoanalysis and the Quest for Truth," *St. Vladimir's Theological Quarterly* 34.4 (1990), 356-60.

munion with him may not be that ultimate goal which gives purpose to the entire dialogue. Christianity must always pass beyond "mental health" and the crisis orientation.

We have seen individual elements of this method being used by the director, including an effort to enable a person to reflect upon his or her life: the director and directee together examine the latter's life-story for persons and events whose influences remain active in the present. They take note of guilt — both appropriate and inappropriate. They examine the passions of instinct with which the directee is struggling. They penetrate the inner depths to establish the relationship between the directee's perception and behavior. They do not, however, fall into the typical habit of interpreting a person's perception and behavior as always resulting from wrong treatment by others — allogenically. In psychoanalysis' most radical interpretation, the patient need only remove the barriers which keep him or her a victim in order to allow the free expression of pressing wishes and instincts. This removes the neuroses which bind him and effects a cure. While such an effect may be realized by this method in some circumstances, it cannot provide the proper basis for practicing spiritual direction.

Can we then, from all we have examined, establish a usable model for this practice, ideally one which will place spiritual direction in relationship with other modern forms of counsel? Dyckman and Carroll's "clarifying scheme"[54] is both compatible with the tradition of the elder and modern science and can readily be endorsed:

| | | **Known** *Directee* | **Unknown** |
|---|---|---|---|
| ***Director*** | **Known** | 1. Arena of free activity | 3. Blind side |
| | **Unknown** | 2. Secret self | 4. Subconscious / Unconscious |

54. Dyckman and Carroll, *Inviting the Mystic*, 28.

*a. The arena of free activity*

In this area are things known to both the director and the directee. And here most of the dialogue in spiritual direction takes place, since it is readily available to both. It is a "comfort zone," the contents of which can be comfortably discussed. This zone will naturally *expand* as the dialogue proceeds and the directee is stretched to grow. Room for expansion is possible either downward into the directee's "secret self," hitherto unrevealed to the director, and/or into the "blind side" about which he or she knows nothing, but which the director understands. As the arena of free activity "stretches" into the "hard areas" of life, the directee will increasingly come to grips with the operations of perceptions (motivations), behavior, and ultimately the patterns of actions which he has been taking. All of this promotes healing and growth.

*b. The "secret self"*

Here reside the "skeletons" in the directee's closet. Here are the things usually viewed as dark and negative — anger, revenge, envy, etc. — not easily shared with others. I do not, with Dyckman and Carroll, regard exploring this area as a means merely to "let the secret self become more acceptable" (which sounds like "approval" of any behavior) but, through the confession *(exomologēsis)* of authentic guilts, to initiate the movement of *metanoia.* This requires an atmosphere of trust between directee and director — the director must do the "accepting" — in order for there to be a willingness to surrender. The directee will have to "die" to the protective devices which he or she has used to disguise the "secret." Once explicated, the force of these issues is often diminished, and the person is able to open up to God's love, given in response to prayers for forgiveness. Digging away at this "secret self" is much the same as turning over the compost heap — new life comes forth only after death.

*c. The "blind side"*

Here are those elements in the directee's life which the *director* — and perhaps *others* — sees, but he or she *fails* to notice. Through lack of insight, he acts without restraint. Much of what we have said about the "secret self" will also apply here. The difference lies in the fact that very often the "blind side" contains one's highest gifts and most positive virtues. As the director observes these contents moving into the free arena of discussion, he can encourage the practice of specific virtues. We often need someone to help us see our goodness, the best traits which we overlook or deny. As the "blind side" is objectified and interpreted by the director, growth and healing are promoted — and we are reminded that spiritual direction operates on the "whole" person, never just one's positive or negative aspects.

### *d. The subconscious or unconscious*

Here reside the truly complex matters in a person's life which lie beneath the surface of consciousness. Here is an area which the director will not be comfortable in entering, and may not prove particularly helpful in interpreting, even when the directee is able to bring them into the content of the dialogue. Here, in an aura of mystery, however, God is free to operate, as the record of the scriptures clearly shows, in the myriad of dreams, visions, uncontrolled thoughts, etc., which he utilized for his own purposes. Respecting the mystery, the director should not even *dare* to address these matters unless they are most obvious and coincide with the full content of the directee's life-story.[55] He or she must know that it exists, but should generally avoid interpretation. Rather, dialogue should focus upon what *can* be realized in the conscious realms and on seeking to bring both the "secret self" and the "blind side" evermore into the consciousness. Since any person is comprised of things conscious and things unconscious — and these two are interrelated — any positive change in one's conscious life can be expected to effect positive change in the unconscious.

55. An example of the obvious connection between one's dreams and one's present life context can be found in my own life story. My late wife underwent a radical series of chemotherapy treatments for cancer. She lost her hair before my eyes — a very traumatic, emotional occurrence. Soon afterward I dreamt in a most vivid way that I had lost my own hair and gone bald. I understood this to be my means of identifying with her agony. Even *that* interpretation of the dream was unnecessary, since I already knew on the most conscious level how deeply I was empathizing with her. The life context was obvious, and only when this is the case should the spiritual director comment upon it. Otherwise, it is best not to interpret dreams.

## Epilogue

Early in this chapter we pointed to the folly of proposing a distinctly "Christian" psychology, which is no more possible than a distinctly Christian economics or a distinctly Christian politics. No form of "statecraft" — be it of society, or of the soul, or of economics, or of psychology — can in and of itself yield up the Christian person. Indeed, any school, any theory, any model — even if it labels itself "Christian" — which pretends to reveal in and of itself the "meaning of life" is a delusion. This must be said, since much of psychology believes that it can weave true meaning and virtue out of human nature apart from communion with God — and this only perverts the truth about human nature. Method *is* important. Had we ended this study without turning to the operational elements of the practice itself, we would surely have short-circuited our efforts at reawakening this ministry for today. In our concern for leading directees deeper into communion with God, we have sought to draw insights from psychology without pretending that it can itself become "religion," and have ever been aware that the meaning of life lies beyond any given method, beyond even the very infrastructures of human life.

# 5 Appendix: Practitioners of Spiritual Direction

It is fitting that we close our study with a look at some exemplary practitioners of spiritual direction. In order to present a well-rounded picture, we shall use two from the ancient tradition, St. John Chrysostom and St. Augustine, and two from modern times, Alexander Elchaninov and St. John of Kronstadt.

## 1. St. John Chrysostom as Spiritual Director

St. John Chrysostom wrote a number of letters of spiritual direction, of which we shall draw on *A Letter to a Young Widow* and *Letters to Olympias.*[1] In the first work, we see both the role which writing plays in spiritual direction and how a crisis can be integrated into the more comprehensive, ongoing process of ministry. We see a director sensitive to the turmoil in a young widow's life. Invited into her life-story, he enters with this tender counsel:

> Since they who are stricken with sorrow ought not to spend their entire time in mourning and tears, but to make good provision also for the healing of their wounds . . . it is a good thing to listen to words of consolation. [121]

1. Both can be found in English translations in NPNF, vol. 9. The number following each direct quotation refers to the page in this version.

A "thunderbolt has fallen"; the widow has gone through the first step of grief which all experience after loss — "shock." During this period, Chrysostom realizes she can learn very little, and so he remains a largely silent "soul-friend." Later, as the therapy of grief progresses, his gift of discernment tells him that the time proper for silence has passed and the time for speaking about her loss has arrived. "While the storm was still severe," he says, he had refrained from saying anything that might "add fuel to the flame." Now he is prepared to enter the various dimensions of her being.

He confronts head-on the issues of her youth and suffering, her security and wealth (her late husband having obviously been wealthy), and finally, her sexuality and affection. In each case he shows clear empathy for her. His manner of confrontation is neither lecture nor monologue, but is born of a careful listening to her tribulation. It makes clear how attuned Chrysostom is to his "theological roots," for he relates her specific predicament to the calamity of fallen human life in general. He is also attuned to the milieu in which she lives — a time of pervasive moral corruption under the reign of the Emperor Theodosius; reversals suffered in the war with the Goths were producing many new widows in a condition similar to the directee's. He warns her against falling into the kind of self-pity, gloom, despondency, and reckless indifference which characterize nonbelievers (pagans); she is a Christian, he reminds her, and Christians are never to lose hope. She is to "see through" the present tragedy and make it work *for* her in the hope of acquiring eternal life. She should not be taken *by* the situation, but should seize hold of it, own it, use it in order to grow — to grow precisely because it has happened.

In his series of four *Letters to Olympias,* the same director addresses a deaconess and heir to a great fortune. She had married at age sixteen and been tragically widowed at eighteen. She was lavish in contributing to the Church's ministry to the sick and the poor, to the point that the Emperor Theodosius took note and decided to divert some of the wealth to his own purposes by arranging her marriage to a young Spaniard. Chrysostom's general advice to her is, again, to hope in the Gospel, but he applies this counsel to her two primary areas of concern: the right use of wealth and ecclesiastical abuses.

On the first point, he risks the anger of the bishops and clergy by warning her against indiscriminate liberality — even toward the Church; for wealth is a trust given by God and should be used discreetly. On the second point, he first seeks to clarify why Olympias is "sorrowful and dejected" concerning the Church. "Is it," he inquires, "because of the fierce black storm which has overtaken the Church?" He confesses that "I do not abandon the hope of better things, considering who is the pilot of all this," and advises that she drop her concerns for the "transitory and perishable," and confront the one thing which is truly terrible — sin. All evil and injustice should be referred to the Christ of the Gospel, who also suffered "railings, insults, reproaches, and gibes inflicted by the enemy." We must deal as God himself deals: "He does not put down evils at the outset." Nevertheless, despite what we humans might think, it is "God himself who orders all things according to his inscrutable wisdom." The director confronts his spiritual daughter with the one true Christian task she faces in the present context: to "reckon up" the misfortunes of this world (the form of which is passing away) against the eternal world of glory to come, of which we presently have a foretaste. He encourages her: "divert your mind from despondency and derive much consolation" from this task of "reckoning up."

Chrysostom's letters reveal a spiritual director who constantly calls upon the witness of the Gospel and applies its message and examples to specific human situations, most vividly in the correspondence with Olympias. In the *Letter to a Young Widow* he displays the methodological elements of empathy, discernment in calibrating the time of direction, and challenging his directee to transform with the help of God one of the darkest elements in human life into light. In both cases the modern spiritual director should not fail to see the careful interplay between *what* the "Golden-Tongued" said and *how* he said it.

## 2. The Blessed Augustine as Spiritual Director

Our second practitioner from antiquity is a Western father. Although Eastern Christians might find faults with much of his pure theology,[2] as a spiritual director he set forth clearly the methodological principles

2. See Fr. Seraphim Rose, *The Place of Blessed Augustine in the Orthodox Church* (Platina, CA: St. Herman's Press, n.d.).

which guided his direction. These are found in his *Letter 266*,[3] written some time after the year 395 to a young woman named Florentina who had sought his counsel. For purposes of clarity we will divide the letter into three parts: "The Master as Pupil," "A Movement toward Freedom," and "Christ as the Interior Teacher."

a. *The Master as Pupil.* "I am not offering myself," Augustine begins, "as an accomplished teacher [*doctor perfectus*], but as one who should progress with those whom he is called to enlighten" (266.2). They both must be aware of the scope of their relationship. The directee knew that she needed guidance before she sought out a director; he knows that he is what we have elsewhere termed "a companion who responds." From his other writings we know that Augustine was acutely aware of what progression meant: ever more profound love for God and neighbor, striving for inner healing, growing in knowledge of the Gospels. In short, he realized that he would always remain a "pupil." He advises Florentina from the start not to approach him as though he has reached his final destination spiritually and thus is able to guide her from the summit. His ministry is both a special calling and a challenge to his humility: "because the teacher must necessarily hold a higher position, he or she must necessarily avoid pride"; otherwise the relationship could become one of superior/subject. He warns Florentina that he will have to exert a conscious effort to avoid this plunge into pride. Without humility he also fears he will not be able to listen well enough. At the very beginning of spiritual direction, she needs to be warned against false expectations, and he against self-delusion.

b. *A Movement toward Freedom.* The director also makes clear, even before the relationship begins, that the goal of the relationship is *her* freedom:

> Certainly, in the very matters that I happen to have knowledge of, I would desire to have you already acquainted with, rather than be in need of me, for we should not wish others to be ignorant so that we might teach them what we know. It is better if we are all disciples of God (Jn. 6.45; Is. 54.13).

She is to be free enough to be directed by the Lord, to be his disciple. As the relationship develops, Florentina is to grow more and more

3. English translation in the series *Fathers of the Church: A New Translation*, vol. 32.

capable of listening to and depending on the Spirit as he directs her. The astute practitioner here confronts the subtle issue of "power" between any director and directee. Direction can be given in such a way as to leave the directee forever dependent, unfree, and spiritually immature.

c. *Christ the Interior Teacher.* Augustine would probably have used the term "spiritual director" very sparingly in relation to himself or his fellow practitioners, for he is most clear that "what we bestow upon you is not our own; we draw it from [the Lord's] storeroom." There is ultimately only one spiritual director — the Lord Jesus Christ. When describing his action within the hearts of Christians, Augustine frequently uses the expression *magister interior.* If a given director is to have an impact, it must be in the service of the Lord and through his grace, as he writes to Florentina:

> Take it for absolutely certain that even if you can learn something from me that is good, your true Master will always be the Interior Master of the interior person. It is he who enables you to understand in the depth of your being, the truth of what is said to you. For he who plants is nothing, nor he who waters, but everything comes from God who gives increase.

Here he echoes St. John Chrysostom, quoted earlier. The director must discern what the Lord wants him to teach and how he wants him to guide. He must not allow himself to "get in the way" of the work of the Interior Master. He must view himself as a servant of that more fundamental relationship.

From the beginning, St. Augustine invites Florentina to focus on discovering "in the depths of her being" the presence of this Interior Master. This will require a proper prayer life, interior silence, and an openness — a receptivity — to the call that will emerge from her depths. This call will not be a demand to "Listen to me" on the director's part, but an invitation, "Let us *together* listen to the Lord." He too is called to interior openness and receptivity, lest he be unable to listen with her.

St. Augustine would doubtless invite modern-day spiritual directors to imitate his concerns for humility in approaching this awesome task — those without it are truly dangerous — and to make the commitment to grow inwardly as we assist others in their spiritual search. He confirms all that we have been saying about the common goal of the *inner way.*

### 3. Fr. Elchaninov and St. John of Kronstadt as Spiritual Directors

That spiritual direction can be practiced in relatively modern times is shown in the last two practitioners we will study, and we will limit ourselves strictly to the narrow subject, since each could be viewed much more broadly with profit.

Fr. Elchaninov reminds us that we will necessarily have to deal with certain "blocks" to the natural growth which God "implanted" in every person. One of these is the error of always expecting "flawless achievements," either by ourselves or by others. When this happens, the directee can easily become "irritated," and even fall into ἀθημία [*athēmia:* "despair"]. We read:

> Typical of the errors which lead to depression, to wrong evaluations, is . . . the idea that here on earth . . . there can be flawless achievements on our part, and on the part of other men, in our human relationships. Consequently, we expect of ourselves the perfection of sanctity and are disheartened when, in our holiest moments, we discover in our hearts impurity, vainglory, duplicity; we are irritated when men we had considered flawless prove to be cowardly, malicious, untruthful; we despair when we see in God's own Church schisms, disputes, jealousies, envy — the unleashing storm of human passions.[4]

For Fr. Elchaninov as for St. John Chrysostom, spiritual direction must be rooted in the dynamic of Christian hope; despondency can only cripple. We can always change, convert, grow better; therefore, we must hope. To grow and to be healed are rooted in this human capacity for change, as St. Gregory of Nyssa writes:

> In truth the finest aspect of our mutability is the possibility of growth in good; and this capacity for improvement transforms the soul, as it changes, more into the divine.[5]

The directee must recognize that both good and evil are truly part of life; one must deal with both, and therefore must constantly exercise discernment, the "mother of all virtues." Abba Evagrios in his *Praktikos*

4. *Diary of a Russian Priest,* 51.
5. In *From Glory to Glory,* 83-84.

states simply: "The good and bad that we meet in life can aid both virtues and vices. It is the task of good judgment to use them to further the first and to frustrate the second."[6]

St. John of Kronstadt's contribution to our final picture of spiritual direction in practice is the reminder that in this life, *temptation* is with us to stay. It will inevitably form a part of every dialogue:

> The Lord allows the enemy to tempt us in order to prove us, in order to strengthen our spiritual powers in our struggle against the enemy, and so that we ourselves may see more clearly towards what our heart inclines, whether it inclines to patience, hope, and love and in general to virtue, or to irritability, incredulity, murmuring, blasphemy, malice, and despair. Therefore, we must not be despondent . . . knowing that all these are indispensable in the order of our spiritual life, that by these the Lord is proving us . . . and how can this be if we have no temptations?[7]

When tempted we have the opportunity to "prove ourselves" by transforming — through our own free choice — the bad into the good. Temptations can strengthen us. The modern-day spiritual director should always encourage his directees to see and hold fast to this truth rather than to accept that happenings and circumstances are merely accidental. We should view everything that comes our way as an opportunity given us by God to prove ourselves. Fr. Elchaninov echoes this succinctly: "Nothing in life is accidental. Whoever believes in accident does not believe in God."[8]

When good and evil in whatever form are brought into the dialogue of spiritual direction, whether they are occurring within the directee or between him- or herself and others, good must be made to come out of evil. The director must aim at a transformation in the directee's perception and behavior and use the crisis for growth. For this to happen, however, struggle is required. One cannot sit back in a slothful, "woe-is-me" manner, on the brink of self-pity and expect anything positive to happen. The pastor of Kronstadt writes:

> Therefore, labour and activity are indispensable for all. Life without activity is not life, but something monstrous — a sort of phantom of

6. *Ibid.*, 88, 38.
7. *My Life in Christ,* 58.
8. *Diary of a Russian Priest,* 101.

life. This is why it is the duty of every man to fight continually and persistently against slothfulness. "Unto everyone that hath shall be given, and he shall have abundance; but from him that hath not, shall be taken away even that which he hath."[9]

The last two Russian priests whose insights close out our work remind us that the effort to direct people toward healing and growth will exact a price. The director cannot afford to forget his own limitations and sinfulness. There is an echo here of St. Isaac of Syria, who reminded us near the start of this book that the director as companion has nothing to give which he did not first receive from God. The director is an instrument of the Holy Spirit, God's surrogate. Unlike the ultimate director, he is not perfect, as St. John of Kronstadt makes clear to everyone who would enter the *inner way:*

> God has not made the angels who are holy . . . to be your mediators . . . but men who, like you, are burdened with weaknesses and sins and who, therefore, are indulgent to your weaknesses and errings which are the same in you as in them.[10]

## Epilogue

To the witness of the practitioners of spiritual direction whom we have so briefly studied in this chapter, we add three "sayings" from the elders of the desert before we say our own "Amen." Every spiritual director must remember:

> A brother who has sinned was turned out of the church by the priest; Abba Bessarion got up and went with him, saying, "I, too, am a sinner."[11]

> A brother of Scetis committed a fault. A council was called to which Abba Moses was invited, but he refused to go to it. Then the priest sent someone to say to him, "Come, for everyone is waiting for you."

9. *My Life in Christ,* 129.
10. Quoted in Bishop Alexander, *Father John of Kronstadt,* 57.
11. *Desert Christians,* 42.

> So he got up and went. He took a leaking jug, filled it with water and carried it with him. The others came out to meet him and said to him, "What is this, Father?" The old man said to them, "My sins run out behind me, and I do not see them, and today I am coming to judge the errors of another." When they heard that, they said no more to the brother but forgave him.[12]

> And because of your own weakness, have sympathy with your brother and give thanks that you have found a starting place for forgiveness, that you may be forgiven by God for your many and greater faults.[13]

It is fitting that we end where we began, with the wisdom of the elders. May their spirit soon be reawakened today, for the time is late and we cannot — any one of us or the Church as a whole — afford to waste any more time in setting out "firmly to tread the *inner way.*"

12. *Ibid.,* 138.

13. Dorotheus of Gaza, *Discourses and Sayings,* ed. E. Rozanne Elder (Kalamazoo, MI: Cistercian Publications, 1970), 238.